CASUAL TIES

Penguin Modern Poets 4 (1963)

Birth of a Shark (1964)

A Christ of the Ice-Floes (1966)

Penguin Modern European Poets: Sándor Weöres and Ferenc Juhász (1970)

Firebreak (1971)

Where the Arrow Falls (1974)

Casual Ties (1983, 2010)

Other Names for the Heart: New and Selected Poems 1964-1984 (1985)

Figure of Eight: New Poems and Selected Translations (1987)

Figure of Eight (1988)

Child Eating Snow (1994)

Solo With Grazing Deer (2001)

Departures: Selected Poems (2003)

Asterisks (2007)

The Boy Who Changed into a Stag Clamors at the Gate of Secrets (2010)

To Build My Shadow a Fire: The Poetry and Translations of David Wevill (2010)

CASUAL TIES

David Wevill

Portland & Salt Lake City

Copyright ©1983, 2010 by David Wevill

Printed in the United States of America

Cover art: Cecilia Yang, *Bird of Four Chambers (Sparrow)*, 2009. Ink drawing. Copyright ©Cecilia Yang. Courtesy of the artist.

Cover design: Michael McGriff

Wevill, David, 1935-

ISBN-13: 978-1-935635-00-0 (pbk. : alk. paper)
ISBN-10: 1-9356-3500-X

Originally published by Curbstone Publishing Company in 1983.

FIRST TAVERN BOOKS EDITION

98765432 First Printing

TAVERN BOOKS
Portland & Salt Lake City
www.tavernbooks.com

CONTENTS

11   THE WALL

13   THEY THAT HUNT YOU

15   THE CITY OF GOD

17   THE BIG LIST

19   BIRTHDAY

21   ANTIGUA MORELOS

22   NOTES FOR A LECTURE

25   THE BODY EMITS AUTUMN WIND

27   BEING ABSENT

29   NUMBER

31   FAMILY

33   TELEPHONE

35   BABYLON

37   BOY

39   SNAKE

41   THE MAIL

43   PIED PIPER

46   FALLING ASLEEP AT *APOCALYPSE NOW*

49   FOUR DAYS

52   ON THE MOUNTAIN

55   FORMALITIES

56   HOUSEBREAKER

59   PENCIL SKETCH

62   TALKING

64   ORPHEUS

65   SALVAGE

68   TRIANGLE

72   TWO THOUGHTS

76   THE TEXT

78   RING OF BONE

79   TIGER TIGER

80   PRELUDE TO AN ENDING

83   A FIRST DRAWING

109   *ABOUT THE AUTHOR*

for the loved ones & the ghosts

Let us imagine a first drawing, which decrees the death of a man.

–Borges

The longer one hesitates outside the door, the more one becomes a stranger.

–Kafka

CASUAL TIES

A man at night walks up to a wall at a place where he believes there is a door. But he bumps his nose on hard wall and steps back. I was wrong about the place in the wall where the door is, he says. I'll try again farther along.

He tries another place and bumps his nose on the wall. Wrong again, he says, rubbing his nose. I must use my hands and think more. I must measure this wall with my hands and arms to find the place where there is a door.

He does this, five or six times, then seventeen and eighteen times, until his hands are raw and no longer sensitive and his arms ache from reaching out. I was wrong about the length of this wall, he says, stepping back to think. I will crawl the length of the wall, brushing it with my left side until I find the place where there is a door.

He crawls the length of the wall until the clothing on his left side is rubbed threadbare, but he has found no door. Now my right side, he says, and starts off crawling along the wall. It is the same result. The man gets up, his clothing falling off him. I was wrong about there being a door, he says. This wall must be climbed. But how high is the wall?

He jumps up against the wall trying to touch its top. He fails to find a top to the wall at this place. He jumps up, here and there, higher and higher, seventeen and eighteen times, until his naked chest is scraped raw. There is no top to this wall, he says, and no door. There are no fingerholds to help me climb. But the wall goes in two directions and must have two ends. I will walk to the end on my left and go around the wall.

But he can't find the place in that direction where the wall ends. So he walks back to look for the place where it must end on his right. Again he fails. The wall is circular, he says. I've been at this exact place before, these are the remains of my clothes. To reach the other side you need to have always been there. Or wait until the sun comes up and shout until somebody hears and comes and rescues you. But is there anyone over there?

It is quiet, and now the sun is coming up. I see, he says. The door I remember is my shadow on the wall. There is no way up or out. But I can get to know myself for the rest of my life, and, with patience, scrape out a small hole in the wall with my finger, and mate with my shadow, engender myself again and again in my shadow.

They that hunt you know two things about you: your location and your name. Knowing your location, they can always find your name. Knowing your name, they can always locate you.

You are free to move about in the world as an unlocated name until your name locates you. You are free to stand still in the world as an unnamed location, until your location names you. Either of these might happen at any moment. They are not an either but a both.

Your change of name has not helped. Your change of location has got you nowhere. You are still what you are and will be taxed as such. Your long list of unpaid parking fines will spell out your name, retrospectively, and point to where you are this very moment. The children you leave behind you, if any, will lead them to the door you think you closed forever, the house whose number you changed at night when you thought no one was watching. Your lost mail has your name and knows where to find you.

This is the law. You are your own law, but this is the law. The law is the mask of the god with eyes but no other features. The eyes are empty. The eyes require your eyes to make them see. The sightless mask is hunting your eyes even now. Give, give generously.

It is for your own good. Your good is their goodness, you will be rewarded. You will be allowed, at times, to wear their mask, to fill its empty eyes with your eyes, to hunt for others as they hunt for you. The feeling of power, though occasional, will make it seem worthwhile. In between the times of power you can laugh, dance, sing, and play the fool you are. They are responsible and will take care of the others. You have no need to feel afraid. Fear is what brought you to this. Now you are cured.

Smile then. Exercise yourself in contentment. You are neither still nor moving, nameless or named. Your name and whereabouts are known to them who possess them by right. They are on loan to you until the time comes to recall them and reassign them to another who even now is being prepared to assume your name and place, your fear and ecstasy, your dread of living and dying.

Love him as you love yourself. Love them who made this possible. Love is generous. Love is to give to the hunter what he asks. Be freed by this. Go forth, be glad, and multiply.

Your dreams are the landlocked onion domes of a city you never visited. There is no water for miles. It is a child's drawing. But that shimmer of heat in the air is time past, hovering, unaccounted for: is dead breath haunting the possibility of this place which is your paradise, decay of body, health and sickness of its parts: your memory.

Wherever you go now, this perfectly preserved ruin is your future. Wars collide in history and are never settled. You are the magnanimous computer, the inhuman scanning device on the South China Sea looking for survivors. Nothing and no one is excluded from your dreams, they gather at the city gate with outstretched hands crying to be let in. But you their master neither live nor rule here.

You are more like them than the god they appeal to. The great gate is locked, except at night when your body spirits you into itself, age being your key. A particle of your self, metastatic, dangerous, wanders the streets looking for a doorway, a place to settle, and there is none. You do not know yourself. You do not know the others who search for you.

What you have loved is what happened to them, the parts of you no surgery can heal. On a bed in Mexico in 1934, two naked bodies entwining in soft brown light. They might both be women: the faces are hidden and it is too dark to tell. In this city there are such darkened rooms if you can find them, and you will recognize the occupants. They are what you have been and cannot touch again. Someone took a picture of you while you weren't there. Memory is erotic. Pornography is the meaningless act of the moment. The bodies appeal to you to break their embrace, or to share it. But you can't touch them.

So this woman, dressed in a black sequined dress and wearing no underclothes, is dragged across the floor by a man. He lifts her up in his arms, and she begins laughing, farting, louder and louder farts. He is angry now and throws her down. He forces some medicine down her, she screams and kicks against it. The medicine affects her bowels, and she begins defecating helplessly, soiling herself and the man who holds her down, screaming and kicking against him. She is beaten then, she is humiliated. She is quiet under the weight of her torturer's body, his will. The dream ends, the doorway is passed. This is history. The distant city of domes under shimmering light is the same.

But there has to be some answer. Weeks, maybe months later, the same doorway repeats itself. The woman wearing a black sequined dress lies on the floor, her dress pulled down to her waist. Five men kneel around her. They soothe her, stroke her body, and one reaches down to touch the soiled place between her legs. She lies there, defeated and at peace with the others, with the moment. Her bachelors have stripped her bare, and she has given them excrement for love. There is nothing left now to give or take.

The people hammer at the city gate. They want in, they are hungry. There is no future for them outside. The mirage fades. The people gather in little groups. Their faces are hidden behind newspapers. I read the print at a distance and cannot make out one word of what they are thinking.

The other day a scrap of paper crawled in my direction, wanting an immediate answer. I said, what answer can I give, I only live here. It said, your life is at stake, your life is the answer I know already, which you are reluctant to give me. Paper, I said, in that case, go and give the answer you know already to whoever sent you, why bother me? The answer might be wrong, said the paper. Also, it must come from you, to show you are alive and not just a name on the big list. What is the big list, I asked. It is the record of all that has ever happened, said the paper, and I am its messenger. The answer is long, I said, it is very long. Are you sure you are big enough to carry it? The answer is in point form, said the paper. It must be short, very short, so that the big list does not become a nightmare of proliferating details, making you seem more important than you are. Your answer must make you look like all the others, but not so much like the others that you cannot be distinguished from their answers. Scrap of paper, I said, get fucked. That will do for length, said the paper. But as for content, it is extremely prejudicial to your case. The big list is serious. It is so serious it never smiles. Scrap of paper, I said, why are we playing this game? The answer you already have is the one the big list sent to you for me to repeat. Why invent another? The big list needs help, it said. The big list has been crying all day at its desk waiting for you to respond. Are you trying to tell me the big list has feelings, I said, it actually cares? No, said the scrap of paper, the big list hasn't a care in the world. But it is incomplete without your answer, it is *big-minus-one*, which is the sort of negative attitude it cannot tolerate. Help the big list. Help to make it whole. Paper, I said again, give the big list the answer you have already, the answer it knows. I will, said the scrap of paper. The answer is, you are dead. You are dead and your name will be erased from the list. Then the big list will be complete again. The big list will be complete and you will be dead. I will tell the big list that. Yes, I will tell the big list. Now crumple me up in a ball and throw me in your wastebasket. Say I couldn't find you. Say you never saw me before in your life.

I walk backward into the time it takes to become my body. There are incidents here I can only imagine now: a gun left lying on a library table, no one there, the air filled with words read or left unopened. The journey in quest of the Grail is now a journey in search of a murderer who might be one of you. If the victim could speak he would say, I did it; open me, the words, the evidence, are there to read.

It was always my intention to create a riddle of what I am, to express it or suppress it, as I have done. Someone else will get into trouble for this. It is my way of involving you, or one of you, in my body which you have disowned, calling it not your own.

A little further on down the table, there is a pile of books. Two are empty notebooks. The other two are books, and I have written one of them: I leave you to guess which. One window has been left open, to suggest I left that way: exited, as they say now, putting the stress on a written word you see above doors, rather than the body that passed through the door. I can't imagine what these clues will mean to you.

I am in this empty library and am part of its emptiness: invisible, but continually whispering to you, through a thousand closed covers on the shelves. You look at those covers and you feel despair. Where do you start, which book do you take down? Because every start is a commitment, however mistaken. And as you begin reading, one after another, at random, a pattern will begin to form around you, a body, which is not your own.

It will develop a head, arms, legs, genitals, blood, lymph,

organs, skin, and a hand will reach out from it and take the gun. The gun might be empty, like the two notebooks. Or it might be loaded, like the two books, one of which I wrote myself.

It is not my purpose to help you. The fact that neither of us is here makes me think we are looking for each other: or for another who doesn't exist, or is a hand reaching for a gun. Who is going to fill the empty notebooks? Who is going to read the unopened books? Someone will have to close the open window and turn out the lights.

I walk backward into the time it takes to become my body. The door closes in front of me, I walk away, and someone goes in. I try and stop him but it is too late, I am walking away. I cannot return now to see who was curious, or who was simply mistaken and chose the wrong door.

I am far away now. I hear a shot, and feel a burning in my stomach. Someone comes running towards me, bleeding and clutching his stomach. We collide, we fall together, and there is nothing there.

The young Mexican boy speaks perfect English and is reading Sartre on his own. We should adopt him, I say. But these are revolutionary times: this is not in fact the present. Leave him be, you say, because what he is about to become has not yet happened, we are intruders from the future, the dark colors of this place are of thirty, forty years ago. There is blood to be shed here in some cause, which you will read about in some book many years from now when you are old enough to call this boy a child, precocious, with a bitter and honest destiny ahead of him. This boy is important. Leave him be. It is the professor in you that wishes to change things.

As we walk away we taste our own death, which is years behind and ahead of us. The dark organic colors of this Mexican town burn bone-white at noon, but this is nighttime. The camera we brought does not record our confusion as to the time: but the boy smiles behind his book, he jokes about philosophy, his eyes know our humor, his eyes accept us and tell us we should not be afraid. There is no theory as to how his life will end, or how ours will begin. It is time to go home. In the mountains they are cutting cane by torchlight as he reads to them his words.

We are older children now, and understand. What we make happen is an altered thought, to comfort us in our age, to impel us to forget a night dream where a boy is reading a book, whose words enter his blood and make him smile for his country and its people. We are backward and scattered. Our eyes reach down and lift words, like weights of iron and stone. We run and run and the flesh falls off us like butter. We are in perfect training for nothing important, but to kill our dreams.

Notes for a Lecture

Because the night is an outcast, tells stories about how little you belong, it is your true home. You return there unwillingly. There are better things to be done by daylight, things of importance. Those who live by night are failures in the eye of the sun. They are the unborn, whose messages seldom reach the light. Baudelaire and a few others. His poem goes like this:

The Owls

Beneath the black yews that hide them
the owls take up their stations.
Their eyes flash red. Like strange
visitor gods, they meditate.

Nothing moves. They wait there
until, the flattened sun now
pushed under by shadows,
the dark takes over.

From their posture, the wise learn
to shy clear of this world's
turbulence & restlessness—

men, maddened by shadows that pass
bearing always the punishment
of wanting some place else

In the same year that book was published was born Ferdinand de Saussure, who spoke of a language of signs: and the year before,

Sigmund Freud, who spoke of a language of signs. They were sun people who reached into the outcast night and stole handfuls of its black fire. They spoke of our failure to know. They did not speak of our need to bury what we know, in order to return to the seedbed of knowledge. As a dog does, or a squirrel in the fall. Thus we confuse our appetite for facts with our need to dream, our success with our desires. And bureaucracies confuse success with desire: success with failure. Those who belong succeed in belonging. Those who fail to belong succeed in being outcasts: and it is important not to confuse the night with the day, one success or failure with the other, one pain with the other pain. These are images, this is a language of signs.

My father worked with facts and figures. He was born in July, a Leo, and was troubled all his life to be a good man. He was a successful man who later in life walked in his sleep, crying and muttering to himself and stumbling over chairs. The night was his enemy, and made him behave like King Lear and the Fool. He loved his wife and his wife died. He loved his children and his children left. He died alone the day before we came to him. These are images, this is a language of signs.

You are oppressed by those who let their tragedies harden them into disciplined belongers. To them the night is a bitter weapon, an instrument for cutting and hacking things into hard angles of light. Forgetting is an art, remembering is a gift. Denise Levertov is a poet. Her poem goes like this:

After I had cut off my hands
and grown new ones

something my former hands had longed for
came and asked to be rocked.

After my plucked out eyes
had withered, and new ones grown

something my former eyes had wept for
came asking to be pitied.

You think you can make it work for you, this cycle of day and night. Where you draw your energy from is the hand you must pay. Where you draw your sight from is the eye you must look into. These things are difficult. How are they done? You must fail and fail and fail in order to be yourself. In the Inner Chapters of Chuang Tsu there are these words:

Such men as Hu Pu Chieh, Wu Kang, Po I,
Shu Chi, Chi Tsu, Hsu Yu, Chi To, and Shen
Tu Ti all lost their lives by doing the
bidding of others. They tried to act in ways
that were natural to others but not natural
to themselves.

Owls, hands, eyes, intrusions, lives. They are outcasts, they are sleepwalkers. These are images, this is a language of signs.

The body emits autumn wind. Decline and decay of things. Futile to imagine time-space of past in present. What happens when trees wither and leaves fall? The body emits autumn wind.

This flatulence is catching. The koan says one must accept the four seasons of life: that the body passes through them, but one's thoughts lag behind or race ahead. The young inexperienced mind does not know what to do with the old expert body, which has always known the world for what it is. Backward and forward moves the scan of memory and future. Two legs walk forward but one is always behind.

One meditates: and the anus, the passage of death, expels dead air. That which we no longer want, but increasingly are. And, as with Yeats, more physical as age comes on: the angry air surrounds us with our smell, and our young minds are offended. Wives and children laugh, but strangers keep their distance. A dog farts, its tail twitches, it walks away from itself, it circles itself, to escape.

Who is this clown we wear beneath the seat of our pants? He speaks out of turn. His humor is deeper than ours: older, darker. Autumn wind from the north, and the geese flying south down river: that is his vision of God, and perhaps mine. But our language is not the same. His vowels come out deep and round or clean and sharp. Mine stutter and hesitate, the consonants hedge against truth. He says in one word what this page is trying to say. He has foreknowledge, while these words, in their effort to know, lag behind or race forward, in an effort to escape his smell, to accomplish their immortality outside the limits of air, of autumn wind.

Old fartface, I say, keep your secrets to yourself. But I am his secret. This elevated discussion is an effort to explain what he says so simply: the secrets I keep from my friends, in order to keep my friends, which they share and keep to themselves, in order to keep me, and keep their distance. This lovely autumn weather we're having enters one as a chill, and leaves as a blast of heat. Don't mind my smell, I say, it's this friend I'm stuck with. He knows it all but hasn't changed since the day we were born, and is likely to have the last word when all words fail. You won't find this is Eckermann's life of Goethe, when the dying man cried for light. Not on your life.

The anus is not the appropriate passage for the transcendent soul. That is the top of the head, where the spirit leaks through, under proper guidance, dissociated from memory and words, purified of all smell. Immortals hold their noses where they go. Praise them, but let your asshole speak to you.

Where I am not is what begins to happen. I am a master of conclusions, sitting where I am, a receiver of accomplished facts, products, whose beginnings are beyond me. That girl who was married yesterday is not born yet. On an assembly line in Detroit, someone drops a wrench onto sheet metal. That sound comes to me as a poem, will come to me as a poem, when I hear it. This is the power you notice in someone who is not all there. It is not a power but a being absent: a remotion of essential particles, waiting to leap together at the sound of a word.

The word could be any word. The annunciation could be any moment. A dream reveals itself in the strange way someone begins behaving when you say: "cobalt." He might begin to mutter: "color, mineral, mother, sky" and break out in a sweat as if from cancer remembered or anticipated. This doll has lost an eye, and the eye was blue. The child no longer remembers the eye: it is a one-eyed doll and always was. Blue eyes got married yesterday. What color will our child's eyes be? The Polish worker in Detroit picks up his wrench and remembers how blue the sky looked over ruined Warsaw. The word is out of control. What begins to happen does not take place.

A kitten is dying again on the back porch. Several kittens have died this year, we don't know why. They become wobbly, torpid, unable to feed or move: they die in tiny convulsions with their heads stretched up and back. Something in their mother or the place is transmitted to them, or fails to be transmitted, and they die. The word is an antigen or a germ. Its beginning is beyond me, but its end is at my feet. I say, there is nothing I can do; but the word "do" becomes part of this sentence: the thing is done. It is a sentence of death. The sentence of a witness of the end who is not there when the event begins to happen.

The world is crying for milk. It is time to feed. It is raining and the smell of food is everywhere, it breathes out of the earth, in waves, convulsions, spasms. Food of life, food of death, food of word. Word as it comes to you long ago formed from its conception, whose witness you are, to use or not at will, to recreate a pattern that has ended or might end with you, in your hands, in the syllable you set yourself to find: a heartbeat weak or strong, beginning, continuing, waiting for its end.

Where I am not is what ceases to happen at last.

The number I am thinking of is a number between six and seven. Do you understand me?

Yes. But I can't guess which number it is. Is it a fraction?

No, it is a number. I want you to try and imagine that number, to understand what I mean by that number, what that number means.

You are playing games with me. My choice is between infinity and nothing. That is no choice at all, but you demand an answer.

Yes I demand an answer. Take as much time as you want, and tell me the number I have in my mind.

I haven't enough time to do what you demand. I'd rather risk a wild guess, a series of wild guesses, than try and get it right.

In that case you might hit upon it by chance, but you could never prove to me that that is the number I have in mind: and I would be under no obligation to tell you if you're right.

In that case, whatever number I guess is as good as the number you have in mind. As that number would never be revealed to me, I would be neither right nor wrong. In effect there would be no number, only an infinity of equal possibilities, bounded by your silence.

Yes and no. The fact is, there would always be a number you failed to guess, a number I know which you would never know you knew: a permanent hole in the universe, shifting always, into which you would try to poke your finger, without success.

This is intolerable. Can't we agree that there is a number which is both known and unknown, and which we can share between us more or less equally, in the harmony that this implies?

That would be a misunderstanding. The giving, the generosity, would be all on my side. You would share what I know, without knowing it, and I would share your ignorance. The number in my mind would begin to fester from lack of recognition. Have pity on the number that needs friends.

Look, I would be the number's friend if I had some way of knowing the number. You ask me to take on trust that the number I guess is not the number you have in mind. And if you were to tell me my guess was right, I'd have to take it on trust that the number I'd guessed was the number you have in mind. Either way there is and is not a number, unless we can agree on a number and name it.

You are a fool, I think. How can we agree on something I know and you don't? I refuse to play your game.

I refuse to play yours.

Look, the number I have in mind is giving me a headache. Be human and cooperate. Help me.

I have no way of helping you unless you help me. Get up off the floor. Please stop clutching your head and writhing on the floor. I'll guess the number. I tell you I'll guess it. The number is—O god. Now I will never know.

The son ranges widely. When the son comes out the father goes in, and vice versa. When the son marries he marries the father's world: and when the father returns he reclaims the world both he and the son are wedded to. They have this in common, though they never meet.

Here is the story of someone who went wrong. The fact that she went at all is a miracle: everything about her said, don't go. But go she did, and didn't she go, once she went. There are better ways to live than to die. To reduce yourself to an idea which has no place in human thought: to be unredeemable, a suicide, expressed now by those who think they have the language to explain you better than your act could. But I have missed the story. A life to be described in shadows we take to be facts. A commonness in us all that occurs in the dark, in the stomach of Cronos, to be vomited up again and crawl away on all fours in the rain, with no words to describe what happened to us, only the idea of it fixed forever, terrifying, and reaching out for other hands, to prove we are able.

Sons and fathers: daughters sons and fathers: wives. A head detached, floating above its spine, like the lower case 'i'. As, by degrees, one grows detached through memory and memory's failure from the stories whose identities we salvage only by will: a poem unlike any other, but not different enough, because what would make it distinct falls between the words, is the words which might have been there instead: the numbers, the dates. When the son comes out the father goes in. Only the wife and mother knows them both. Their wants are written in pencil on a little pad beside her bed. She keeps their details separate, though the natures of the two amount to one. If ever the two become confused, she must turn out the light and lie down in the dark alone.

Which is why that ambulance has come to that door, and two men run in and disappear inside that house. They emerge with a third one between them, a hyphen joining them yet holding them apart, and drive off into the night crying for help: the siren howling and the lights beating like the idea of a pulse, recovered and lost.

Too early yet to tell what the day will bring.

But the nerves you get up with are what make things happen. They cannot be soothed or fooled. What am I to accomplish, asked the man eating a meager breakfast of toast. This is a day like any other. I am not a bureaucrat, but they have my number. Any moment now there will be a phone call. Something urgent has happened in my absence which requires my absence to pretend it is there. Resist, I tell my mirror. But my mirror is my number already being dialed. It has located my reflection: which is what they were waiting for.

Too late, the man steps back and hides his face in his hands. In the dark of his hands there is a landscape filled with night: rivers and red sandstone cliffs, where stunted people move about, with implements and goats, among tiny fires. For a second or two he watches them. There's a shout. He has been seen. They are coming for him with spears, running up the cliffs of his shut hands towards his eyes. The hands drop. His reflection receives him back. The phone rings.

He does not answer the phone. The phone rings. He does not answer the phone. The phone begins to talk. It rehearses his childhood, his life. Number by number it recounts his innumerable lives: cell after cell responds as it is called, remembered. He is summoned now to go to the source of the call: the phone's reflection at the other end of the long wire, where someone sits with growing patience, telling the lengthening story to which he listens, ring after ring, of the one who must eventually be present, whose life will have preceded him to this place where it is already recorded.

Who is about to enter the door now.

Forced into the world late, without enough difficult experience until much later, for which there is not enough knowledge except anxiety of childhood, remembered, but not understood: there having been no clear reason then, there being little now, beyond the need to account for what went wrong, and continues to go wrong, as at heart the heart does not change but simply grows older, learns to avoid, learns change but not how to change—itself, others, events—speaking well but encumbered by its eloquence: until the last word questions everything that was said, and is answered by silence appropriate to its ignorance. *Om.*

Men and women struggling in a room trying to agree on a policy. Lights on and the windows shut, though the evening sun comes into the room and colors naturally the unnatural inmate skins of talkers and listeners burning with desire to do the wise thing at last: but not knowing how: each in his and her own wisdom, not knowing how. Forced late into the knowledge that each one is and always has been wise: but they have no wisdom in common, nothing to go on. The motion is on the table. Get it off the table. The motion is on the floor. *Oh god it's on my shoe.* Scrape the motion off on your neighbor. Let him stink of the motion, it's not mine. The motion goes around the room looking for its mother or father, a breast, a penis, recognized by none. If the motion is adopted it will grow to become a policy. No one likes a policy, it sounds too much like police. The motion is disowned. It will die from lack of milk and body heat. Bury it. Another will be born with better luck. We are in a permanent disorder of fear, and there is another time for everything: a better time in a better world in a better future. All things bright and beautiful, all creatures great and small. All things wise and wonderful, the Lord God made them all.

Freud did not think people made mistakes. But Freud might have been wrong. Each one in himself is not mistaken. But, among others, each becomes the other's mistake: is mistaken in the other and by the other, until he is wholly other and not himself, at the moment of decision, not there, not in his right mind, or in anyone's mind. Men and women struggling in a room at sunset trying to be good. I will vote yes. I will vote no. I will abstain. He who votes yes accepts the motion. He who votes no has other things in mind. He who abstains dislikes the motion and fears the other things in other minds. "Since ignorance is increasing…" said Baudelaire, and never completed the thought.

A hundred ways to make your hubby feel he is loved. Take out a policy in his name and go to bed with it. Business as usual, monkey, funny, or otherwise, you and he will both feel renewed. Make a motion. Make a pretty motion. The prettier the motion, the more it will be loved, the fewer ugly looks it will get as it passes into policy, gracefully trailing its perfume past the noses of its admirers, the jaded, the impotent, the young and full of desire, who line its path as it passes, gently, into middle age and redundancy, and another meeting is called in this same room at sunset to declare it medically dead, and another is chosen, denied, or abstained from. This is the way we do our hair. This is the way to Babylon. This is the way we are.

The boy wants to grow old. He sees it coming every autumn, falling around him from above, everywhere he walks: reading but not understanding the parable of patience and fear, with the sound of old chicken bones or crayfish shells underfoot: his shadow companion with which he plays, not yet his successor.

There is a limit to being old in imagination. Height to be reached, words gathering around him like pubic hair: an itch to replace what is there with what is there but out of reach: a friendship with trees, with treetops full of hands and girls' eyes waiting to open and take him in. Books of old romance tell him how this is done. He will outgrow them until the old stories return to tell him he has won or lost, but never again how.

How is what an observer sees who was not there. The boy is seen to grow old. He makes love to everything he touches or imagines: he gathers age from everything he lies with and tries to penetrate. As he hardens these things grow soft, they become too easy, they declare they are outgrown. Later he will regret abandoning them for other forms too hard to penetrate, which will become his obsession. In turning to find them again he will discover his impotence: as now he holds it in his hand and begs it to give him some peace.

October comes, and everything runs toward a burning field where a scarecrow dances in the smoke. People gather at fires, tears melt out of dry lives, eyes burn. The boy is older though he does not know it. He stands naked among children who laugh at his wrinkled genitals and run off. Older women come and speak to him about his mother. They offer themselves to him in reminiscences of how he used to play with toys when they were neighbors. One by one he takes them into the woods, and they lie still, waiting, while he gathers leaves and scatters them over their bodies. When they are covered he lies on each heap of leaves in turn and dreams that he is on fire. When he is done he urinates on the heaps of hot ash and walks away. The woods close behind him.

He has forgotten his words. He has lost the power to speak, and begins counting. As the numbers mount he finds he cannot remember his age, and doesn't know where to stop. There are voices in his head, coming as the numbers come, like a tape recorder run quickly in reverse: which are people speaking to him of years they have known him, each one an imprecise memory into which he sweated and threw his seed, not thinking, not there, in imagination or fact. The boy wants badly. The boy wants. But the boy is not now or then.

The boy is there on the step. He is eating an apple. He throws away the core. The apple core lies in the street, turning yellow, turning brown. The marks of his teeth in the core are hard to trace. Something will eat the core when the boy is gone. Nothing depends on the boy who is no longer there. Who is succeeded in memory by this moment in time long gone and numbers still to come, or words heard clearly.

Once in upper Burma driving through a village there was a group of men around a brushpile beating at it with sticks. Suddenly a large stick-like thing shot out of the brush at shoulder height and scattered the men. They began beating at the ground and followed it into a paddy, where the snake escaped and the men stopped, afraid to go further.

I stopped the car and got out. I looked out across the paddy where the wind had begun to blow: miles of solid green stretching east to blue hills of post-monsoon autumn. The snake had gone there. Its absence was the single point of pressure in the landscape: a long horizontal line running, curling and resting, in no direction, in all directions where my eyes spread, like a fact you can't point to, a knowledge you can't accept. The men went back chattering and exclaiming. A radio started up with a wailing love song. Women with water jars on their heads, men with work to do, and the snake listening.

Snake vibrations were with me all day in the car, on the long winding road up through the hills. I was going nowhere in particular, just going, on a day free of teaching, wherever the hills took me, with no one but myself to think about, and the snake. I saw other snakes but not that snake. They would cross the road like distorted shadows, writhings of road pattern, and disappear into the trees. All kinds of snakes, none close enough to identify, with my poor knowledge. But the day which had started free of any thought was now crisscrossed with snake-thoughts: it lay under the snake sign, a sign I had not chosen but couldn't escape. They were right to think a snake can be a god.

You can't beat a snake with a stick and hope to win. That is bad politics. The snake will take the shape opposite to the stick and evade the beater's will which is straight and thoughtless and hard. To catch or kill a snake you must dance with its shape until your dance and the snake's dance entwine, and suddenly you have him, or he has you: it must come to that. There is always that risk, and those who avoid it get fooled.

Nights I slept with snake and ate snake three meals a day. Snake became my intestine and my mate. Snake was my excrement, my urine was venom. When I came to myself again, I had acquired a habit I have not lost.

You must learn my dance and not expect to win.

Every day the mail takes a little longer to come. Some days the mail doesn't come at all. But the mail that comes is not the mail you are waiting for.

What you are waiting for is not the mail but the thought behind the mail. The inexpressible thought which no envelope can contain: but which must come to you in a form you recognize, and can open and say: "It is here at last." No other kind of mail is worth opening. It is closed forever in its sender's mind.

If you were to befriend the mailman, you could talk with him about this problem. He would understand. What letters the mailman gets must be trivial imitations of the letters he thinks he delivers. Mailmen, excepting Charles Bukowski, cannot afford to grow attached to words. The addresses they read, each no bigger than a *haiku*, and none larger than a *tanka*, clip their interest short. Behind these precious few words there is one unopened thought, inexpressible and without end, which is the meaning of the mailman's life and yours. You share this secret in complete ignorance of what it is.

To be caught waiting by your mailbox is worse than being found pissing behind a tree. The image will remain of an empty man, who hopes for more than the world can possibly hold. Total silence is better, total maillessness. Let the signs come to you as they occur, as random as falling leaves, or the sudden sight of eyes watching you from a bench.

But avoid those eyes, before they find out who you are and where you live. Those eyes might write to you or fail to write: and

every day, a little longer each day, and some days forever, you will
be waiting to understand what it is you are waiting for: which is the
torment of knowing that all possibilities are only apparent—that
any mark, any mark at all will do, in the eye of the sun.

Why does the single engine Cessna circle round and round in the dark above the river valley, without lights. What is the brown Ford station wagon doing pulled off on the left beside the still unfinished highway. Who is in trouble out there, beyond my insomnia that listens to these things and tries to make a pattern for a dream that will not come, outside the circle of the clock face, within the circle of the plane circling overhead, looking for the place in the world where it can land.

Marijuana. The word strikes fear into the tough policeman's thighs of Jean Genet's imagination. En masse the children file out of their high schools, two abreast, hand in hand, following the sweet notes of the smoke flute, and the mountain closes behind them. Sports equipment lies rotting in the locker rooms and the expensive gymnasia of our invested future: the ghosts of mothers and fathers wander the landscape night and day with tracker dogs, and nature receives them back. The Dow Jones Average mutters to itself like a telephone left off the hook and forgotten. One by one the electric lights plink out. Night descends, black as in the Middle Ages, to the cry of imaginary wolves in the forest of the Ardennes. God circles overhead, or it is Beelzebub the fly, looking for a place in the world where he can land his stash and melt away into omniscient absence.

Four hundred pounds of top grade stuff for the furnaces of Moloch. Or is it the children again. Only two out of every five reached maturity in the Middle Ages. Do two out of five Americans reach maturity? We grow bigger each generation, we are giants, we frighten people. We commit violence, we witness violence: our fiction is filled with violence we neither witness nor commit but dream or lie awake planning it. Give us peace. Give me sleep. The single engine Cessna circles round and round without lights. I am piloting it, it is my responsibility, I must not sleep. Or it will land in the wolfish circle of police cars, and its hide will be shredded and torn by the spearmint freshened teeth of the sheriff's men. Four hundred pounds of someone's flesh and blood, the size of a good stag, in or out of season.

Or is it the children? It is the one lame child who was too slow to follow, and the mountain shut in his face? He had a story to tell but no one believed him. What story will we believe: what story will we cease to believe. Dope and the power to learn mathematics don't go together. Mathematics is the root of what we believe. Dope depends on the mathematics of money. The mathematics of money is dope is what we believe. We have sniffed each others' exhausts long enough. As a social activity it stinks but is permissible. As a solitary vice in a locked garage it takes you farther, farther than you want to go. I must fly my little single engine plane with care, so it will not crash into the mountain where the children have gone, to find what peace they can.

But I am wrong about that. The mountain is hollow. Mature people live in it now, with supplies, weapons, and computers. A control room, an alternative government, a bed and a red button for the leader, in case something happens. And we, the rest of us, man, woman and child, are that lame boy who didn't make it in time, hobbling back on his crutches to tell a story no one will believe, about something he has seen which has not yet happened, but which is why he has not slept since then, and lies listening to a single engine Cessna circling overhead, above the heads of his own children whose dreams, unlike their sleep, are as fragile as bubbles.

He had gone deaf and could only see the explosions, the helicopters crashing, the men and women screaming with open mouths as silent as flowers. The beauty and horror of the scene was its silence, and the wonderful colors were pollinations of a world gone deaf, vegetating in a peace beyond fear. The earth shook but there was no reason. It was his heart shaking the earth: and he was standing on his heart, which had fallen from him like a snow cone from a paper cup, a patch of wet, the raspberry color gone, absorbed in the white dust at his feet.

He had almost gone to sleep during the final scene. He didn't know why. He had waited all night for these words, that actor's face. But the world had become a dream, and the words he could no longer hear were part of it. Death, and death's jokes, had become a mumbling staring eye—the face of an actor so familiar in this role that at some deeper level the words became his own words, and he dozed with them, repeating them in his mouth. The screen went black, the silence became total. Then the colors returned.

All his life had been a war fought at a distance beyond his age, his place, his obligation. Born in the *kurai tanima,* the "dark valley" of the thirties in Japan, and finally, past acceptable age, asked to register his name with a draft board in Texas, among names born while he was trying out for the position of end on the high school football team: though neither of these was his real country, where he had not lived now for more years than these names were old, he'd kept his own distance. War then was a dream as familiar as the place of his heart in his body. The words spoken by the actor were from his own heart, melting down, beneath his feet, amidst the litter on the theater floor, in the dust, his deafness, the bright colors that came and went, like flames seen and not seen through a parallax of trees as one walks in a forest.

The problem is, one refuses to stop being a child, and being a child doesn't pay. Meditations on war and war's images: the blunt ferocity of soft colors and sounds: how close the nightmare is to making one sleep, dreaming what others remember, giving them back their memories as dreams: the director shouting to his actors to perform, perform—and this is their war, their real war. The swastika spins and is a vortex. *Svastí*: well-being, luck. *Sú* good, + *astí*: being. And it is feminine, the cross spinning clockwise with broken limbs, the rotors of a helicopter homing in on blood, like a bedlam mosquito. The action is so natural it induces sleep. The action is so natural children imitate it as they dance in the wind. Every drop of blood from a cut is dedicated to the fear of dreaming something worse.

They walked out of the movie theater hand in hand, the south wind blowing luminous clouds low overhead. They walked on broken glass in the dark, and drove out over it, home, upriver, where the night lamp and the books waited. I won't be able to sleep after this, she said. And he: We've slept already. Let's hope the children don't wake up too early. I'm invited to have nightmares stronger than my own, which is what truth is about, and power, and that is why I refuse to learn but must wait indefinitely for further proof that something happened to others I did not know about, at a time and in a place I was not watching closely enough. I know the story I have just been told. I knew it so well I fell asleep before it ended.

Dozed, with the actor's face and words in my brain, a bedtime story for a child whose wars have always been dreams.

And he could not have predicted this. He needed more than anything to be told the small, hostile facts of an unmediated world, which neither theory nor imagination could shape or beautify into a tolerable horror, too like the colors, the twists of his own mind. The power of art is greater than the sum of its victims. Its victims are small, silent and colorless: friable earth shelled to white dust, paddies thrown back centuries to waste tracts visited by useless monsoon rains, and no survivors of that world where thirty million dollars of good American celluloid might buy the fortune of a rice seed. And this is not what he felt either, detached from what he imagined the facts to be, in that far away country without lights, his mind being more like that which had made this apocalypse, so like it that he had not remained awake until the end, but slept back into himself, confident of the world he was asked to enter and accept. Would he have done it differently? He had not the knowledge. He was secure.

The poetics of reality go beyond fear. They go beyond suffering, but do not resolve it. They are the luxury of being human, and humanity's imagined end. Approach an animal, and it will run, or come to you, as it perceives you are its enemy or friend. It might attack you for both reasons, and you cannot predict this, or dream a way around it. He had not knowledge but he knew the dream. And she was right. The night had been stolen from her and turned into day, vivid and terrible, beyond her power to compose it in her own way. They neither of them slept. Nor did the bodies rotting in the jungle find a way into their hearts, for fear of waking them.

Four Days

He had taken twenty or thirty pink Seconal tablets, he couldn't tell how many, and lay down on the couch gripping the small silver handled Burmese knife, in case he found the courage to cut his way out. He was raving and the words came out of no language he'd ever spoken, not in his memory at least, but were sounds he understood. He was out of cigarettes, and had failed to go to the bank that day, a Friday, and there was nothing in the place to drink, no supper he felt like cooking. These were the conditions under which he began to take his own life: the conditions, not the causes. It was late at night. The carved wooden Buddha he had talked to every day watched him silently from over by the window, its smile an indifferent sneer, its woodenness beyond words now.

Later, lying awake among others trying to sleep in the public ward, being visited by nurses keeping him awake, his brain alive, among others injured in other ways, some old, some young, convalescing or reaching their end: he knew the fantastic peace of having done something. He drifted on the river between worlds, rescued but not yet returned: pure consciousness, without fear. The details of his life and the reasons for his death had gone away. He was alone at last, without self or people. He had no identity or form beyond knowing he was at peace and alive, and there was no obligation but to keep awake, to feel the touch of the young nurse's hand, to speak to her as Adam spoke to Eve, in words beyond his memory, of intimacy at the river's edge. No one had a name. Nothing was named, and his brain was not ready yet. It was a Saturday, early, before sunrise.

To wake among strangers was the greatest healing. In the day or so he was there he learned their stories, but kept his secret. He learned their stories so he would not have to face the one who visited him asking why, the one too intimate, the one never far enough from himself, who later went the way he had almost gone, and was not found in time. To return to normal only applies to body temperature. Between people, and within the self, the stories can be adjusted, addresses kept or changed, fictions carried forward to their true or false values, because there is nothing to go on, no rules, no principle, beyond partial attachment or partial solitude—ideograms one learns to write, with their different meanings, different combinations, poorly or with skill. Let's talk about the blackbirds in the cornfields. I walk forward, and I walk back. What takes me forward, what makes me go back? Rhythm and return. The trouble with a poem is it does not know its power. It is written and spoken too lightly, its relationships are incalculable. It returns to the world from the dead, and reaches to the dead in the other world, infecting all it touches with the illusion of the act of returning alive. It was Sunday evening. A taxi took them home.

But a shadow lay on Primrose Hill, which had been their shared face. The ability to see double, the light in the trees and the trees' dark nature underneath, in the grass or the sheen of polished car metal, makeup around a young salesgirl's eyes, the quality of light and dark in a book at different places in its pages regardless of plot, the double face of that druid hill in North London, covered with picnickers, did not come back to him for many years until he had evaded every question his crisis asked him, then and over the years, to this sunlit Wednesday morning in late October, smoking too much, but with fewer shadows, and deeper ones. The trouble with a father is he must know his own mind. And to know it he must leave it alone, as it is, so his children can climb on it and play the games they know are other lives they have, between worlds and of both worlds, where questions are meaningless.

The windfall tax kept the professor from thinking about the weeklong visit of Shakespearean actors. They perform and are gone and the news returns reminding us that the price of tickets is far too high, and that translators are soon to arrive to talk about their specialties, in rooms filled with languages, poems still to be drilled for at high cost, like desert oil from sheikdoms. In a jacket patterned by dust falling from high bookshelves, he meditates, and his glasses mist over with obscure longing. He meditates, and his hands shape a football: something to hold, like a bomb, or a baby, or a lifetime of work he can understand. Something to throw to someone and receive back in a perfect parabola of recognition: from one's hands to someone's hands, no footnotes required. From someone's hands back to one's hands, like a door opening to reveal a thirty years gone friend, not the shadows that pass the frosted glass of the never opening door he waits behind, counting, thinking of the high cost of girls whose faces he has on a list, whose names he can't get right.

In the Fibonacci series of numbers, twenty-one numbers take you from one to ten thousand nine hundred forty-six. It is a great gain with a small investment. A great leap, a godlike progress, like leaping in a dream over a darkened central European landscape filled with spies and counterspies, yourself aware of the danger, but immune. A homecoming to a closed room, where a professor meditates these words: "We were too late for the gods and too early for being; whose poem, already begun, is being." The man who wrote those words lived on a mountain some of the time and wore peasant's clothes, perhaps to remind himself that thought is earthbound and smells of sheep manure and mountain wind, and to avoid talk, where talk is possible, among the numbers of things. The poem already begun depends upon the professor's sense of smell, its shadows passing behind frosted glass, male, female, animal: the odor of words and not the priest-like footnotes of the word, the magnum opus of a football shaped from air and thrown to no one. We are praised by our abstractions and must call the mountain 'magic,' for there is no mountain in our lives, but something in the shape of a professor, a man, waiting to be asked the question that will occupy him for the rest of his days, be it in numbers or in words, the question, the obsession. We are too late for Heidegger and too early for death, whose poem, already begun, is eating us.

One professor at a time falls from the tree of knowledge and is swept into piles. The piles are gathered up before the wind scatters them, or the piles are left too long and the wind comes and scatters them—must this metaphor go on? The bookshelves pass through seasons: spring, summer, autumn, winter. The books are never the same though they look the same. They are moments of touch, moments when something was touched, put down, remembered, forgotten, to return, like a childhood scar when the hair begins to recede. We are aware of starvation in ourselves, and its metaphor, its image, in far off Asia. There is not enough blood to share. There are not enough words with which to regret the withheld blood, or celebrate the professor's meditation on the lovely skirts of girls whose heads he occupies with unmentionable nouns, a seed here, a seed there, a generation pregnant with his name. He is too late for the poem and too early for them: whose being, already begun, is in search of gods.

The professor leaves his office to the tune of a band playing a football march, gripping his books tightly so he won't fumble. He is off to buy a Shakespeare ticket, though the troupe of actors has left now, and there are only translators, translators talking in rooms, about the high cost of foreign exchange, between a Chinese poem and a poem in German meditated by a dead man who lived on a mountain, and spoke about gods as if they too were words.

When someone is undressing she is naked before you see her nakedness. It is the figure's intention to undress that reveals her. You are watching and know the moment when her movement becomes stillness and the act is done. It is the moment of obsession when you recognize yourself in her, and your heart stops beating, your eyes turn into hands, and the hands are hers.

Housebreaker sits at the top of the world tree throwing boulders down on people's houses. He has always been a child. No one could ever control him, so they gave up trying. They lie in their beds or wander about their kitchens wondering when the sky will crash open above them and they must run for their lives, or die under the sudden weight of whatever they imagine death feels like. Housebreaker plays no favorites and bears no grudges. He is the child who does not graduate into the fragments of adulthood. He has no love or hate, he merely plays.

He is not to be confused with your own children, or with something worse than a god because it has no personality to appeal to, as most gods do, however whimsical. Housebreaker is simply what his name suggests. He has no respect for roofs and walls and whatever inhabits them: they are targets for his boulders, though his aim never improves, and it is quite possible to wake up one morning and find your yard littered with huge rocks that failed to land on your house, and which weren't there the night before. That is after a night raid. A daylight raid is different. Then you can hear the sound of boulders falling from the sky, whether you are an Anatolian shepherd or an executive on the thirtieth floor of your glass office building reckoning up stocks and bonds that might never mature for reasons this story makes clear. If you are a poet, these sounds could be the music of the spheres: and you would be right, because Housebreaker likes his boulders to be as round and smooth as those sacred harmonies the ancients heard.

All efforts to wear hard hats and protective armor have come to nothing. People have moved underground, people have hollowed out mountains to escape Housebreaker's obsessive behavior overhead. The result is claustrophobia, and a greater, more terrifying noise of persistent pounding on the earth above their heads, driving people to madness and even suicide. Quiet prayers have been offered up to everything imaginable, in hopes they will reach Housebreaker's ears. But his ears have not been found, nor his excrement, nor one hair of his distant head. Housebreaker was born not of woman, nor of man's head or thigh. No one knows his shape or size: but his smudged fingerprints, immense but quite human, are found from time to time on boulders that have fallen on lawns of police detectives, physical anthropologists and students of zoology. They agree that we are dealing with a huge baby or possibly a child, unless he is a compound, a chimera, whose other parts are mysterious. People have waited in the oddest places for the longest times, hoping for something to fall from the sky that has never fallen before which might help identify him. As the world tree has never been climbed, no one has seen him, not even from a distance.

Housebreaker remains intact, while our towns, cities, villages and farms are always changing. His effect on the birth rate has been catastrophic, or beneficial, depending on which side of the issue you take. No one wants to raise a child who might look like a spot of raspberry jam in the morning. The death rate among the old has risen too, as no one wants to give shelter to a grandparent, only to have to carry him or her out on a shovel for decent burial at the start of a busy day or at the end of a busy day, in a yard looking like an irregular Stonehenge but without the meaning which that place once had. America and Russia blamed each other, but gave it up after SALT XXIII, when neither could prove that the other was guilty of anything worse than being coy. For a while, earth-moving equipment imported from Texas was used to rearrange the boulders in artistic patterns. But people gave up. They decided to accept a fact whose cause they could not determine but whose effects lay all about them or crashed through their roofs. It is no harder to accept than the fact of death. But it makes it harder to accept life as a fact more certain than a breakfast egg's bad dream between the icebox and the saucepan, eaten in haste before the traffic piles up on the freeways heading in.

Me, I could not live without Housebreaker. I blame him for everything, and consequently I have many good and blameless friends, and no enemies I can identify on the ground. My roof is intact and guaranteed for five more years, and a careful study of Zen has made it possible for the boulders in my garden to be mountains and offshore rocks where spirits live who speak to me quietly of catastrophe and peace in a monotone that harmonizes with the sound of falling air. Occasionally, I wonder about a son I have, or might have had, whose being has escaped me, or mine him, and of whom I am reminded every time a neighbor's roof falls, wondering why mine has been spared, for what purpose of that child's playing hands, which any day or night might reach for my life crying with the impersonal thunder of one forever lost and abandoned, beyond time and repair.

Writing is not a craft, an art, a vocation, or a career. It is an obsession, he said, biting the end of his pencil until it bled. What this pencil has to say is that things wear out: that a thought carried too far, like any physical object, becomes a stub whose body lies sprawled behind it in the words it set down, while the pencil itself, its remainder, is nothing. The blood of the well-used pencil begins to leak into my mouth. I taste it, its sacrifices, its used up purpose, in my mouth which does not speak the words it writes in place of my voice—always silent, always from the head, a story as pointless as a worn-out pencil, but one that must be told every morning my breath wakes me and I am forced to live. When the breathing stops the inner pencil dies. Meanwhile these little wooden soldiers live and die before my time, each one carrying out its purpose, none speaking, as I don't speak, but silently tracing the words which for some reason one does not walk down the street speaking aloud for fear of losing something or being thought insane. It is the silence of this ritual that makes it seem magical, and also suspect. This grip on solid wood, like a giant writing with a fir tree, is my hold on the world. Everything is diminished, must be squeezed into characters small enough to be read easily. The silence of the process is like one animal feeding on another which is still alive, but too far gone to complain. I taste the blood in my mouth, of those things my words feed on. My obsession is with eating whatever I can before my time runs out. I call this communication, if I must. But the fact is I'm hungry.

"You do not give enough of yourself in your writing." No, but I take. And in taking I give back the illusion of giving. "That man has a gift," they say, "for words." But the gift is *of* words, an illusion of giving back what one has taken, in order to create a pattern that will appear to be more than the stolen goods were worth: the things of this world. Magical, as I said, and suspect. Are you fooled or is it I who am fooled? Perhaps the only virtue is to entertain and make people forget that a writer confiscates their minds if he is any good, at least for the while he is present, replacing their own being in the world, with the illusion of his greater being and theirs. "What is he writing about? Has he anything to say, or is he just spinning out words?" And is there a difference?

If you really want to know what happens in the slums of Calcutta, no description will do. Or the best description will leave you with the illusion that you know, but the facts will remain outside your knowledge of the words which are what prevent you from knowing more. The writer has taken away the slums and given you nothing. You have received the slums from the writer and have nothing left to give to the place where the slums remain, beyond your power to touch them with your hands and feet. Mother Teresa's face will tell you what you've missed, but not enough. No prize for peace, the price you pay for peace, by reading or writing words. You are hungry and I am hungry. How can we feed each other, without feeding on each other?

And after all, nothing has happened. I have told you nothing, because I have nothing to tell. It is a sunlit day in Texas, a little before Thanksgiving, and the grass is covered with brown leaves scattered in patterns left by the south wind which has gone. There are children playing outside, but they're my responsibility. They describe themselves as they run, and batter each other with shouts and cries. I could entertain you by describing these things: but they are not part of my hunger, or yours: they are not our obsession. What that is depends upon the bitten end of my pencil, the pattern of my teethmarks in soft wood, as I taste its blood and reach for another pencil to sharpen, and go on with what I was saying, at another time. Like most of us, I am writing my epitaph. A few words here or there might make a difference.

At a time when people still talk about the heart, where have the buffalo gone? I am driving beyond the sound of my own name. I am out here on a highway where the maps are older than the places I come to: always a strange turning that wasn't there, a settlement beginning to grow old as I speed past it, so that the girl of seven playing on her lawn where the settlement begins is that grandmother rocking on her porch at the other end, in a house grown much older, a frame house which had been a ranch-style bungalow with a TV aerial above it as big as a tree, allowing the girl of seven to look at any program she chooses, swept in invisible gusts, like the buffalo, like the wind, across the high plains and into our hearts, a dream which people still talk about as they talk about having a home, whether they are seven or seventy: a heart, a home.

My car is insane, and I must keep talking to it, keep it moving. The way I talk to my car is the way I would talk to my home, if I had one, narrating the way it must keep changing, adding to its mileage or its number of rooms, as its lifeline grows, its family increases, without a break: for to break the story of journey or settlement would stop the heart for the instant it takes death to enter and wreck the car or reclaim the home. We are married and must grow old together. If we fail to grow old we have not lived. We have not passed through that settlement where age happens at once, so suddenly that the settlement is not on our maps before we come to it and not there after we have left. So I keep talking to my car. My life depends upon the words I choose.

I myself am of indeterminate age and avoid mirrors. All, that is, except my driving mirror, which reflects my eyes from time to time as I glance at it: the eyes that never change and appear to be looking backwards even as the highway draws them forward along an infinite thread of grey or black converging at some point never reached, in memory's other space, where give me a home where the buffalo roam is the nursery song I was raised on, heard again in the speed of this car, the stillness of this house. For I am very still sitting here in this vinyl rocking chair, the wheel in my hands, thinking how old I have grown with my house, how young I am about to become when I reach that settlement, where my seven year old bride waits playing on her lawn and settles her walking stick between her legs, in a print dress, peering over her spectacles at a fine line of dust that could be my arrival or my departure. If I can just keep talking it will be all right. I must nurse this thing to a point where I feel I am neither moving nor still: where the map, my heart, fills slowly with the ghosts of unborn buffalo, whose song is the wind beating against my house, buffeting my car with words I haven't found and names of settlements which are born and die as a child's ball rolls into the street and stops.

Why do you not sing for the Thracian women, you who once charmed the animals, the rivers, rocks, and forest? The power you were given cannot change the way time feeds on itself, on you also: a fox roaming in the darkness. For when the music stops nothing has changed. There is only this restlessness, a sense of having been moved but not transformed. Their hunger remains. Your silence is their hunger, and you must keep playing or be eaten alive, a head, a harp, adrift in the river, to be found and buried in the sand. They have acquired a taste for your songs, which they mistake for your body as long as the song remains. But their hunger and your body will outlast the music, and one day, in the silence of its absence, they will strike. It is not good enough to say, I have dreamed of the underworld, I sing for dead Eurydice, only to her. The live ones listening so intently hear only themselves. In the fingered chords and half-imagined words, the gutturals of their own viscera talking, only to themselves. And this is the way with you, too, in spite of your divine gift. You have lost the dimension where things must be as they are. You are neither alive nor dead, but a sound, diminishing to silence as it spreads and fades. So your body opens, note after note dropping as blood. And the nightingales sing, touching dead Eurydice at last, blood for blood, slaking for the last time the thirst of those who circle you and listen, singly, none touching, like ten fingers without a pair of hands. What remains is your name, a word for darkness, the magic found in stones, and the fury of the Thracian women whose eyes you avoid, as they stare with the fixity of leopards at the breathing shadow they thought was Orpheus.

Someone's trailer home is burning. The scene is peaceful. The demon fire works quietly, softly eating out the heart of someone's trailer home is burning, has burnt, is aluminum melted and collapsed, stove burst, mattress smoldering, a few toys and a blackened ceramic vase under scorched trees leaning over what was roof and is now heated air on a peaceful morning in the country. The hoses disappear with the volunteers, the busy leader with a bleeding hand who kicked in the walls, laughs, drives off to breakfast with his children. Someone asks for a name. No one knows the name. No one had seen the trailer home before it happened. Someone mutters, "Someone's mother I think," but no one was there, it happened in someone's absence who is the only one who could care, and lucky for that person, everyone keeps repeating, lucky for that person who should have been there but was not, is not, dead and unrecognizable, but alive and unknown. "Nothing can be salvaged from this mess."

A week later and still no one has come. Where is the person who owns the gutted trailer home? If it is someone's mother, she should care. She may have gone to Idaho for Thanksgiving to visit relatives, children, or friends. How far is Idaho? It is above the snowline now, far north. Will she come back when she hears? No one knows who she is or where she's gone, her identity must be read from the ashes, the shape of a blackened ceramic vase, the size of a burnt mattress, the scorched fingerprints on a blown out stove, a few toys the demon fire left untouched for someone's child when a man's foot kicked through the wall and a rake pulled them out steaming onto the dew-wet grass flattened by boots of the volunteers. Somewhere in this mess a familiar thing she lived with, handled, knew, is the key. The key the demon used to break in and dance in her absence: to begin his dance, his *bal des ardents*, his dance of the flaming ones, the suicidal dance of fire that must be killed, put out, at the height of his frenzy. The woman's lover called but she was gone. He danced his fantasy of their love in her absence and left her his sign for her to read, if and when, whoever she is, she returns to mourn his angry death. It is the fire she will see and not her home, which looks like something dropped from the sky and crushed by the weight of its fall, like a tangled and disordered bed collapsed under the weight of repeated passion, sodden with sweat, the black blood of fire. She will read his sign and her blood will run cold.

Someone's trailer home is burning still. The engines arrive, the volunteers, and no one asks if anyone is at home. The scene is peaceful, a Sunday morning in the country, and some will miss church because of this, this exorcism by water, the hounding of the demon back to liquid ash, in the absence of someone's mother who had forgotten or was ignorant of something elemental and dangerous behind her which danced in the shadows of her kitchen when she was alone and called her name whenever she struck a match to light her stove and cook her simple dinner. Plain and growing older, her memory filled the trailer house with something she wanted but didn't dare ask for, as it was too late, it had to be a conflagration at her age, to warm her, make her feel he had returned: which is what she waited for, and was absent for, when it came. The boot of a volunteer kicks through the wall. A hose scalds the twisted iron bed, smashing fragments of black stuff off the steaming mattress where she lay looking at pictures of her children on the wall, uncertain how her life had been or how it would end, as it has not, not this way, not here, this time. Lucky for her who should have been here, but is not. "Nothing can be salvaged from this mess."

The volunteers have gone. The fire is out. A week later and all the leaves are down around the gutted trailer home, but no one has come. They wash the smell of fire off their hands and faces. The party is over, the party to whom no one was invited, whose hostess no one knows, at a strange house no one even knew was there. They return home to their wives as if from an orgy, sweating, triumphant and spent, unlace their boots and speak of missing church for once, of bacon and eggs and plans to repair the sink before the nights turn freezing and fires have to be kept lit, as this is the country, and these are pioneers. They guess at the possible name of the homeless woman, and the names drift into the names of children and friends, and go no farther. They're stuck. Their day is stuck. There's nothing more to do. "I wonder if she was insured?" The leader puts antiseptic on his cut and goes to the refrigerator for a beer. His wife goes through the clothes in her cupboard, planning for a perfect winter, seeing what can be salvaged and what thrown away.

Someone's trailer home is burning always.

He killed the fourth of his oppressors and was now looking for the fifth, though he wasn't sure that the first three were dead, as the media had kept silent about the murders in an effort perhaps to flush him out, make him overplay his hand, or his nerve.

Now it was Sunday again, the day he usually struck. He was polishing his German .22 target revolver, when it occurred to him that the sun was not at the right place in the sky for what his senses told him was the time. He checked his watch and found his watch had stopped. He stopped polishing the gun, caught in a triangle between the sun, his senses, and his dead watch. He knew that the man he must find stepped out onto his patio at exactly ten o'clock every Sunday morning, stretched and took five deep breaths, and went inside again sliding the glass door shut behind him. The whole sequence took exactly one minute: and that was the minute he had to be there, hiding behind the box hedge, at an angle of eight o'clock to the left and behind the man, six feet away, where he would aim the gun exactly behind the man's left ear, steady it, and pull the trigger. The man would fall, and he would be done with this phase of his life, having acquitted himself in his own defense since there was no justice, no God, no life worth suffering for. The next phase would take care of itself, as this one had done, when a new cast assembled to stand in his sights and fall, in order of their appearance, as this one had. But it was not finished yet. There was something wrong with the time of day.

He thought of calling a neighbor to ask the time. But he hadn't spoken to anyone in over a year, and the surprise of his phone call might stay on in his neighbor's memory and link him, as memory does, obscurely with a killing that took place that morning. He tried to dial the time on his telephone, but got a busy signal. He waited and dialed again, but got no response and gave up. There were no public clocks between his room and his victim's house to set his watch by. The sun was still at a strange low angle to the earth and seemed not to have moved, while his senses told him it was dangerously late and he must get going, must be there the moment the man appeared, his breathing quiet and his hand steady, and do his morning's work: as on the seventh day he also had to rest, his conscience at peace, his work done. He set out walking towards the subdivision one mile west of his room, the gun in his pocket. But his shadow in front of him was too tall, not lying at the proper angle to the low sun, as westward in the morning, eastward at evening: but southwest, as no shadow of this length had ever fallen at any time of day. He looked at his watch and noticed that, taking twelve o'clock as north, the minute hand had stopped in exactly the direction his shadow fell in relation to the sun and that as he walked he was being drawn in that direction himself: not west, where his target waited, but off course, bending gradually southward, towards a part of the city where he knew no one and where he had no business visiting. His shadow was leading him. He tried to correct his course, pull away from his shadow, but found he could not move and was being drawn back, drawn on, along the dark heightened track of his silhouette which seemed like the sun's finger pointing him on, lengthening ahead of him, like a burn mark along which it was possible to walk. His senses told him the sun had still not moved. He tried to turn his head to look at the sun but could not.

He had timed the walk to the man's house at exactly twenty minutes. Now, twenty minutes after he left his room, he stopped. He did not know where he was. He tried moving left, right, backwards, but was held fast. He tried to walk forward, but his shadow had stopped and would not let him move on. He found he could not move his head or his hands. His body was paralyzed. But his senses were awake and were acute. He heard a clock in the city striking ten and saw, behind his eyes, the man slide open the glass door and walk out onto his patio. The man began to stretch; he held the stretch for several seconds, then bent his arms in front like a man rowing a boat, and began his slow, deep breathing, holding each breath as long as he could, spreading his arms slowly outward and sideways as each breath reached its greatest depth, then slowly releasing the air, and bringing his arms forward as the air expired. He did this four times while his assassin stood there, a mile to the south, unable to breathe or move, watching it all, knowing every move and feeling the seconds pass as the sun held him, while his shadow stood like a guard to which he was chained. Then at the fifth breath suddenly the man stiffened and gasped. He clutched his chest, his head, staggered, fell on the patio stone, and lay still. His body and hands relaxed and went soft, the head slackened sideways and the eyes half open fixed on the box hedge a little to the left and behind him. There was no breath. At this moment the other's shadow relaxed its grip, and he moved, he moved and leaned against a wall, and began to breathe. The sun had moved in the sky to a position he recognized. He set his watch at one minute past ten, wound it, and began to walk in the direction of the church clock he had heard strike ten.

Twenty minutes later, walking north, he arrived at what should have been the church but was the man's house. He had wanted to pray, to give thanks, to express his wonder at the miracle that had saved him from having to act. An ambulance was leaving the house as he approached, and a police car was parked in front. He walked in the open front door and out the sliding glass door at the rear onto the patio. He saw the mark of blood on the stone flags and two policeman searching in the box hedge to the left and a little behind him. One of them stood up with a small shiny object in his hand. The two examined it, then noticed him standing there and approached him with it, asking his name and his business there. He tried to run but he was paralyzed. They held him and searched him and found his gun. The gun was fully loaded, but the bullets were the same as the cartridge they had found. They took him in for questioning, but there was nothing he could say that they believed.

A further thought speaks to one that is closer, and the two agree to meet at a point between them, which is not occupied by a central idea. The notion here, at least the feeling, is to collaborate and generate a meaning which will be satisfactory to both of them, filling the space they know as loneliness, a treeless plain of dead grass where words travel in caravans knows as sentences, to protect themselves from attacks by the wild grammatical flaws that afflict all thoughts with primitive and irrational fears.

For generations now all thoughts have been exiles, far from the empire's center where language is worshipped as something pure and sacred, worth preserving, worth human sacrifice and animal blood. Our two thoughts pack provisions for a day's journey across the dangerous plain, each one heading for the other's smoke signal, meaning: "Come, come, let's meet before it's too late." Toward nightfall, as the two thoughts approach each other, each is attacked by a small barbarian hunting party. They survive the attack, but both are seriously wounded, their provisions gone, their natures radically changed by the experience. They crawl towards each other muttering strange sounds, deeper than words, perhaps too deep and far gone to become words even with rest and healing. They collapse into each other's arms and lie there, rubbing together, generating heat, not sexual heat, but contradictory feelings. Like all thoughts they are neuter, neither male nor female. They depend on words to engender meaning: and these two are beyond words, frightened and hurt, poorly expressed and vague.

After a while the closer thought gets up and builds a campfire. Further thought lights it by the friction of two sticks, and they sit by the fire in the now total darkness. Neither can speak so they simply hold hands, glad to be alive, but unsure of their future. As the fire warms them their heads clear, and closer thought speaks.

"Bl-bl-bl-bl-"

Further thought listens, nodding its head, trying to pick up the rhythm.

"Bl-bl-bl-bl-bl-bl-bl-"

Further thought nods and opens its mouth.

"Uddy uddy uddy uddy"

Closer thought joins in.

"Bl-bl-"

"Uddy uddy"

"Bl-"

"Uddy"

"M-m-m-m-m-"

"Mmmmmmmmmmm"

Then both together.

"MESS."

They nod wildly together. They've got it. They've got meaning.

The last syllable leaped together between them, without either's urging it. They have defined their situation and are triumphant. They forget the cold, the threat of the great darkened plain around them, and fall asleep in each other's arms, dreaming of further progress.

When dawn cracks the east horizon of the plain, they get up, stiff with their wounds, and begin foraging. They have forgotten about progress and are hungry and cold. One collects firewood and the other hunts for edible seeds, uttering the strange and gastric sounds of wandering thoughts at a loss for words or nourishment. Though day has replaced night, their situation has not changed, and while they are forced to think further afield, they cannot go beyond the meaning they achieved last night, the complex thought they put together, in words. And neither can yet complete that thought alone: to grasp the bloody mess they are in they must say it together, closer and further thought, one encouraging the other, in that order. Though the sun has risen, the day is not yet won. It will require time and effort to put together even a minimal sentence, let alone a sentence long enough to allow them to move in safety across the plain, with its bad barbarian grammar waiting to leap at them from the tall dead grass, where it is rumored the deadly saber-toothed syntax also abounds, with its insatiable appetite to interfere with thought and kill all logic. Thinking of this, in its mononucleotic way, further thought, returning to the campfire, has an inspiration.

"J-j-j-j-j-" it begins. "J-j-j-aw-aw-aw-aw-eeeee-sssss. Jawwweeeessss. Jaweess. Joyes. Joyes. JOYCE!"

Further thought got it all out by himself. Closer thought is amazed. It joins in, picking up on the first sound, describing its own hunger and anxiety.

"J-j-j-j-j-" it begins. "J-j-j-ay-ay-ay-ay-mmmmm-sssss. Jayyyeeemmmss. Jayeems. Jayems. Jayms. JAMES!

"JOYCE JAMES!" they cry in unison.

They dance around the campfire, backwards, not in the right order, but delighted with themselves. They have developed a complex thought, a magical incantation they cannot understand, but which has made the day, the sun, seem brighter. They think of progress as they munch their seeds, not knowing that they have spoken the words that will prevent all further caravans from crossing the great dead plain of grass safely, or ever again move in any known direction, bearing their commerce of barter and meaning, their nomadic pilgrims, refugees from plague, pillage, and wars, provincial governors heading out for new posts, Ovid and Burton, Mandelstam and Li Po, paired thoughts in exile, dancing around the campfire they have made, dancing, in this leap of time, in the wrong order, further thought first, closer thought behind, chanting their magic formula, enchanted by it, getting it wrong but getting it right, right over the horizon, their circle spinning faster and faster, whirling, smaller, out of sight, and safe at last together, safe and sound, as the wind rises and the great plain stirs from east to west, a solid pelt of grass with nothing on it.

One has been there and one has not. Two might have made it a place, an occasion, to remember. But two were not there: one had to invent the other, so the place and the occasion were fictitious, and what one saw truly with his eyes was his own falsehood, pleading with the wind, the waves, and the gulls to confirm his legend: as Odysseus' legend, lying open on his knees, was confirmed by the ocean, looking east, the early morning sun, at the place he had marked and left open, as if to attract what might come riding in on the waves of this more northern sea at the beginning of his day.

He writes one word in the margin: Open. He waits.

Stillness moves one. Movement holds one still. It is from movement that legends are born. It is in stillness that legends are written. The two make an occasion and a place. What is one up to, thinking he is thinking, unnerved by stillness, unable to move, sitting here at a place where the sun touches the sea, nakedly, without mind: waiting for something to open, for another to appear and call his name.

He closes the book on the word he had written, and waits.

One outwaits one's perfection. One waits and waits to be made incomplete. One is added to one, or one divides and grows: one becomes two, three, four, ten, and loses the godhood of the sun, and is everything under the sun, all things, all systems, all laws, but can never return: can never be that which never leaves itself and so never returns.

He opens the book and writes three words in the margin:

Monad, Nomad, No-man. He waits.

The primal fire, from which all things come, to which all things return. He lights a cigarette and draws a circle in the margin. He touches the tip of the cigarette to the circle, and the circle burns, expands. Its black edge eats the words he had written, eats into the text of the sun, the beginning of his day, and stops for no reason at the O of Odysseus, whose journey is not yet complete, and therefore not fully begun: as one must know the end before he begins: the stillness in the movement of the heart.

He tears out the burnt page and waits.

Mummy, what is that man doing burning all the pages of his book and throwing them into the sea?

RING OF BONE

for Gary Snyder

Here we go, laughing. The way I saw it first made me think I had seen it getting killed, though it got up with a smile on its face and walked off, dusting the seat of its pants. "The pants are not the trousers," I thought to myself. "You can call the trousers the pants. But can you call the pants the trousers?"

I had coffee and thought about the difficulties we have with language. Beside me, a girl was hiccupping into her milk. I thought of my dog eating grass, and said, "Take her outside, she's going to be sick." But they said, "Leave her alone. She's about to become a mother. Don't touch her or the child she bears will be deformed."

I have been on a hunger strike for seventeen days. It was like this all the time the hostage interviews were taking place, I couldn't eat, and whatever I tried to eat came up as propaganda and lies. I have been looking for a young mother with full breasts to help me out. But all I see are trousers walking, or call them pants, getting killed.

I wear my ring of bone around my left wrist and gnaw at it. I am teething again and the bone is as soft as rubber, but it tastes human. They tell me I am going feral. But I say, "No, I'm laughing." My laughter wears trousers and walks with a slight limp. I might adopt a child soon, or a young mother, but certainly not something I could kill by mistaking those words.

The animal that thought itself a tiger scratched its eye out looking at the sun. A one-eyed tiger can still hunt, so this one thought of a smaller weaker creature it could chase and overcome, as its stomach felt hollow, and its mouth burnt from tasting too much breath and air.

That weaker animal ran ahead of it all day. It ran along the tunnel of the tiger's single eye, among the patterns of thought that dappled the floor of this jungle, skittering and flushing other game from the tiger's path, but never getting close to being caught. "This is a problem of perspective," thought the tiger, resting and rubbing its good eye. "I must think myself a second eye, in order to catch this creature I have thought escapes me."

That other eye rose with the moon, but it was blind. The eye was dead and white. It gave the tiger no pain, but it got him nowhere, as eyes go, as this one came. "When you ask for a gift," thought the tiger, "you must specify. Balefully I see that weaker creature stopped ahead of me, waiting for me to resume the chase. I have forgotten all else. I must think of something."

It thought the weaker creature moved. The tiger pounced and caught it, there was no struggle. It chewed, and what it chewed was a damaged eye, an eye that thought to itself as it was being swallowed down, "What insight on the tiger's part to see how close I was to him all the time."

One takes his father's shotgun, cleans and loads it. One tiptoes through the house at night, opening doors. In this bedroom one stands, aiming the gun at two heads sleeping side by side. One waits five minutes and leaves.

Night after night the same ritual with the shotgun and the heads. Nothing wakes up. Nothing notices his coming, his waiting, his going. The two heads dream a future for their son, a past for themselves. The dreams are funneled down two narrow corridors with light at neither end. When they wake he is gone, when he wakes they are gone. Only here, at night, for these few moments, they are together, the two lives held straight and parallel in one's hands. And one imagines them running, running ahead of him over snow or white gypsum desert, in night's monochrome whose darker shadows are like blood.

One might come to his senses. Or she and he might come to their senses, before the sun explodes and leaves new planets burning, spinning, in place of the old ones. Or the gas oven, where mothers and children are led instead of the deep forest, will lure them to its waiting room where the old sit streaming tears of damp winters beside children restless with fever held in mothers' laps which are shapeless easy chairs not places of sex or birth. The waiting continues, the interminable interval between the pulse of heart and that of earth. Nothing grows old here but has always been old. Odysseus' bow and Penelope's tapestry: the shotgun in its rack, the mother's lap unraveled. What act initiates the journey of escape into the story's bitter fulfillment?

He showed no emotion when told why he was being charged. She wept, but could not stop herself or abandon her child to its own life. Night, with its deeper, fatal wisdom, waits to absorb the strength of those who have answers, the strong hearts that find the journey terrifying yet filled with promise of heroic reenactment. And what is life without wit, the sustaining jokes that outnumber the dead, that account for the dead? The need to speak of these things, to prove that speech is more than just an echo of the setting sun. And we go down singing

    deeper. He wept for his lost companions and
    the hall fell silent. Then one rose
    picked up his harp & sang

    & while the tears fell from the guest's remembering eyes
    a light filled the great hall as the singer's words
    told of acts done in the names of gods

    & their breasts were full. Then the guest rose
    & said, I am the one whose deeds you sing of,
    fate brought me to your shore & a kind wind

    sped me like an arrow to your hearts.
    I am the man the gods have blessed with misfortunes.
    My name is…

But dawn comes, and one replaces the shotgun in the gun rack. The stove is lit for coffee, and the people in the waiting room are still waiting, unspeaking, waiting to speak to the one who can relieve them of their need to wait, the one who can return them to the interval which is their lives, in common with the father's dream, the mother's and daughter's dream, and the son's sleeplessness. Night after night after night. And at last, daylight. The dependence on things yet to come. Which is the meaning of one's ungiven name: not nothing, not emptiness. The look backward through the gunsight from the barrel's end.

A First Drawing

Brown before the first big spring rain, moot, lie the rangelands and meadows, scattered with patches of that coarse, tall, silvery grass whose name I'm always forgetting, which crawls partway up the low cropped cedar hills and stops before the rocks take over, making little cairns around the stuntier cedars, with a buzzard or several sailing around the summit to lend perspective. Now the heavy rains have come and the thin soil can't hold its nourishment, it spews in brown flood down the dry creek beds and through small towns and trailer camps that wake to brief nightmare, then shake themselves like a muddy dog and trot off, or get up, stretch, and rebuild. Morning fogs and night fogs. If someone drops a hammer in the valley the sound hits my foot: I wince, curse, turn on the light and look at the clock. It is always late and there is always a noise. I think of people I know lying in their beds and wonder if they think of me, some visiting each other in dreams, like a secret party to which one was not invited, the solution to throw one of your own and see who comes, how they behave in your house: one, you, I, them, a conversation of hammer blows on wood, a radical lovemaking, rhythmic, without the erotica of flesh to absorb the sound of the strokes. Living on a patch of land that tilts, no flat place to walk but the floor of the house, the bed. A habit of leaning, a feeling of sliding, learning to walk again. But what a gift! this being alive, to teach myself to repeat things as they happen again, the cycles of recurrence, the trap and the pattern, the slow walk over old ground, counting the steps from point of rest to point of restlessness, so that my name disappears into other things, which are subject to the weather, its dangers and its blessings, its not quite accurate memory of what it should be doing where and when, wayward like the inca doves but always there, the fluting call of families in the undergrowth or in quick beating flight above the forest floor, where the sun abandons itself among the leavings of what it encouraged to grow up tall, the great orphanage of fallen children returning as food for others willing to try and grow and be broken as is the story, the energy, endless, relentless, too slow for the mind to grasp.

But at night, with only the clock, it comes as fear. The moment when the last birthday really occurs, and you have reached that age, delayed, but quite certain that you are here, and passed like a row of motels your last alternative, too late at night to choose. So, as is often the case when someone lies awake, you are driving a car on and on along a highway made up of many other roads, and the one beside you may not be your licit mate, but one to whom you wish to tell your story, uninterruptedly, as a kind of ballad whose broken phrases permit no tune, no song, but are themselves a magical release from explanations and doubts, a sketching out of a future life that has happened already in enough detail to make the story true. A story involving walls, nightmares, tigers, infidelities, hunters and hunted, libraries, scraps of paper, poems, Mexican villages, assholes, owls, numbers absent and present, guessed or uncertain, mothers, fathers, telephones, committee meetings and snakes, and the letters you compose but never send, the letters you receive but do not read, the brush with suicide, and the need but failure to kill, the apocalypse of the final letter, Omega, Orpheus, salvage from a fire, the comedy of two thoughts meeting, Odysseus home but to die, a ring of bone, a ring of words, of accidents to come as the car races on. At night with only the clock to listen to you, or by day the wind, trying to set out in detail the drama that is not a pure invention if that were possible, but a way of filling in time with pieces of itself that were memory-lapses, as this morning I couldn't even remember your name, but got it, with effort, when your blind face swam towards me across the pillow. And it was the children who came into the room to complain about dresses you'd chosen for them to wear that helped me remember that you are the one in the car in spite of names I choose as alternatives, faces rigid with inexperience, or with their own experience, which is not open to mine. How can you stand this one who has nothing to say but is full of things to say which amount to nothing? The world around us is its own story already told. The rest is like shaking a tree to see what creatures live there by dislodging them, which as a boy I used to do, but as a man I leave them to be imagined. There is no drama in this. And without drama, without the demon playing behind the words, the story can only describe itself and hint at what it might have been, like a cat that eats its litter of kittens, one by one, for no reason you can understand.

"My colleagues leave me cold," said my friend and colleague, and might have meant me too, except that he was talking to me. I sympathize. We are all too busy these days. We have disappeared into our work, which is not our work but our duty to keep busy, as a way of making the machine that feeds us a burden we can all share, a common act of charity and love. So it is difficult to be personal about anything. Those who lapse drift too far back in the wake before the ring can be thrown, and it is past the time for heroics, when one leaping chance, taking you out of yourself, can make a lover or a friend in a moment, or create forever an obligation neither of you can live up to. "The sign of the times is cautious optimism." But it's spring, and my nose takes in the old smells, the exudations of the mother who is not a machine but to whom all machines aspire, even as they violate her while trying to perfect her. I sense a cautious optimism in the night sky, to which I seem to have moved closer, though I've forgotten the names of many stars, memory-points in a heaven which no longer serve me as guides but as patterns of perfection to be gazed at with awe by one who has forgotten his earthly geometry, his ways of walking in his own body, the grace of being in touch with what is his. "When did we last make love?" The body can't answer that question. The mouth can, but doesn't. The act is either an act or it is lost. "Prove to me that we are still in love,"—and that's reasonable, because as life takes so much from us the proofs become harder to act out. The desire is always there, but somehow the acts don't amount to whatever it is the desire asks of us, they are like the stars whose names one does remember, so few in the heavenly scale, attached to nothing but themselves, but they are the only objects you can point to in the sky with confidence, like brief matings on a bed whose scale is time, whose desire and meaning are time. Where is the drama in this? It is too large, amorphous and inert. Better to write an epic about the cut-ants on their hundred yards long journey carrying stolen leaf-parts to some distant hole you can discover with patience. That completes itself, that story works. The nest, the hole, the desire is achieved. Though the whole procession resembles a machine, it takes from the mother and returns to the mother what it takes. What do I take from you that I can return to you? What can I offer you but what I have taken from you, which may have undergone the change of living in my blood but is still, and has always been, yours? Our bodies are bruised not against one another but against emptiness. We desire, I feel, the same thing, but are we the same thing we have desired, so long now, that this earth, this house, these children, are what we have become, are the bodies we have left us to become, finally, ourselves?

This is the final pattern then: not the embodiment, but the completion of these sketches. We do not live in the true southwest, but in this curious trick of history and varied space called Texas, shaped like a child's first effort at drawing a star. A child's first effort at drawing a star can lead to anything. Let us see what happens when we try.

> Each one of the five points
> loses its struggle against
> the contradictory pull of its true &
> near opposites
>
> A star is born
> to frustration. The child has no sense
> of the limits which are
> perfection of form. The plasma star
> crawls in all directions, but is a
>
> star nonetheless with
> five limbs: arms, legs, head. Or
> call it a star, a desire, a

love of form penciled in light
wanting to become what it
fears most: that
which has nowhere further to go

A man in space
a woman in space, a
code of language: how they mate
& reproduce & speak to one another

in earth's permanent song. And
all roads out of this lead into exile
the graveyard of stars where perfect forms
lie scrapped, their edges rusting

making a kind of beauty
an earth-temple of forms returning
from exile to the mother. Where is the light
born that teaches us
to read our failure into another
better star? A child tries again & again

(but there are limits) to achieve
the imaginary face of some thing both
human & perfect. A poem
set to the music of itself, a star
sketched without any effort at all

accompanied by cries, or the silence which is a cry
resembling his body & soul or the teeth of angels.

The comedy of our times is that people are trying too hard
to be funny at the expense of real humor, which is the failure
to maintain seriousness. A poem about a star is not like a child's
drawing of a star, it self-destructs into its own gravity and self-
importance, it turns your attention away from more serious
matters, such as: what follows? A man has woken up on his own
doorstep, and feels the sun shining in his eyes, burning into the
headache he brought home with him and failed to reach his bed
with while the moon was setting. It is the season of spring, a little
later now, and the man feels the dew on his clothes and skin. He
has been somewhere he doesn't remember, with someone he will
never see again. Now he is home, and all he has to do is open the
door and walk in. But there is a problem. He must invent the story
of his absence from home, a story that must sound as if he never
left home but was there all the time: a story so truthful that those
he tells it to become its witnesses, as Odysseus told everyone he
met the most outrageous lies, and was feted for it, and welcomed
home by Penelope and his son Telemachus. It should not require
a hero to bring this off, or an Irishman. But where does the man
begin? Is he confronted by the same wall that kept him prisoner in
the first of these sketches: or has something happened since then
that has taught him how to improvise and so create, for others, a
more convincing self?

So. A man has woken up on the sand, on the shore of his own
native country, though he does not know this yet. He feels the sun

burning into his eyes, burning into the headache of his long voyage home. His body is still in reach of the sea, its shallows wash over him and retreat, bringing in and washing back the scattered pieces of his text, now soaked and illegible: the words of his journey's story he must now remember and repeat without their help. What should be the happy end is now a further and greater ordeal: not merely to have survived all that happened, but to assemble now as facts the elements of a story that occurred to him as a dream whose details some fool, perhaps himself, wrote down and then destroyed in his despair at finding no meaning in the story or too many meanings for him to tell it as one man's account of himself, before witnesses who were not there, his wife and child. The comedy is that he must be entertaining in this, while his bruised, sandy, sea-washed body, his matted hair and sun-blinded eyes, make him feel it more in terms of moral lessons, destiny, and other serious things. How is he to tell his wife about the pig woman and her island brothel? How is he to believe her when she tells him that, in all this time, she hasn't met a man to better him? What is he to tell his teenage son who sits upstairs in his room, polishing his father's twelve-gauge with a kitchen rag? And how is he to open and enter the front door of what he now recognizes, by signs, as his home, and walk in and begin the thing as if he were a long-awaited god returning, in his potency, from the bitter wars of boardrooms and committees, to embrace them both and drive out all their ghosts? His finger traces a star in the dirt on the porch railing. His head is bent, he's thinking something out.

Meanwhile, somewhere, a sentence is forming. Between logic and the empirical falls the Odyssey, falls the imagination.

"When dealing with logic, 'One cannot imagine that' means: one doesn't know what one should imagine here," said Wittgenstein. I can imagine so many things my heart aches with it all. Is that the sentence? Or is that the sentence that says no story, no effort, will do? He comes back to Ithaka to find his car keys where he left them with some loose change on the table in the hallway where the phone is kept. "This dithering leads to nothing but grief," he says, for no reason other than that the thought feels right. Upstairs he hears his wife flushing the toilet, or is it his son.

To have left a wife and son together all night reminds him of other tragedies we have faced, and his mind wanders from the story he is trying to compose to another which he might tell, as a diversion, to deflect the need to explain away from himself and onto the two upstairs, his loved ones. That he does not know his son, that it is not his wife upstairs but his son's mother, makes the story no less difficult to tell. The house looks like his house but it might not be his house, and the loved ones in it are strangers who are loved because they love each other: "his" because they insist on being his, as they need to posses him and be possessed, the obsessive desire for completeness, the three, the family, the triangle: beginning, middle and end. So now he has come to explain why he has been away, and that he has come back to his house perhaps to die and so fulfill some prophecy he never understood.

For I am no longer myself
And my house is not my house.

There are no people in these dreams. There is a man walking

upstairs with a story forming in his head, or a man walking up a rocky Texas hillside in spring, with his eyes, while his car speeds west along the rolling four lane blacktop, and he turns to the one next to him and says, "When did we last make love?" and immediately forgets his question as the landscape changes, flattens and becomes more desertlike, and he is on the upstairs landing now looking into rooms, looking into the empty sockets of his own fear, for clues to the story he is unable to tell. I am here and I am there. If you look for me I will return to ask why. We never leave each other in peace. We never return to each other and find peace. Is that the sentence? Or is there one unwritten yet which is too close to truth to make sense. Who is on trial here anyway, and what is the ordeal? Who or what is it that someone must face and give an account of himself to that will release him gradually or suddenly, into a freedom that is the beginning of the same explanation at another level: the terms of which become more and more symbolic to him, more abstract and therefore desperate, as the pattern becomes known to him, and the energy it takes to fail and fail again at telling the story makes it impossible finally for the story to be told? Unless the story itself, in all its terrifying strength and simplicity, is the stumbling block: his sacred truth and also his obstacle. The man pauses. The beds have not been slept in. Who is in the house?

It is the woman who names her son. No man. The seed of ignorance of his ancestors, born into the stillness which is violence, the world in which he has not yet acted out his personal sound: which is already formed and perfect but not yet formed in his mind and by his mind. To have returned to the stillness of an empty house which is his home is like being born, is like the momentary formation of a stone abridging all the years it takes the heart to stop, like this. Violence may be an act. Or it may be the stillness that prevents him from acting when he knows that there is death in the house but he cannot find it, aware, as he has always been, of the hugger-mugger of life's apparent motives, where he is receptive to every small sign but is helpless to arrange the signs in any decent order and follow them to his longed-for but forgotten goal of resolute accomplishment of self. It is woman who names her son, from whose grace he continues to fall as the questions mount up against the affirmation of his birth and name, which are the first and last complete and unquestionable text he will ever have. So now he begins to play with it, to search for the others he has no way of knowing are here, in hiding, and within reach of his voice, his personal sound, if he can find it. Are they important? Or are they masks of importance, held between his face and the sun?

I abandon the bedrooms and walk down the hall to the bathroom. The door is locked from inside. I tap on it but no one answers. I call out, but my voice is muffled against the wood and no one hears me. There are words gathering to meet me beyond the door as I force it with my knee and shoulder, breaking the lock—words of someone else's story gathering to meet mine, as I am now the questioner, the vacuum into which their story falls, not the narrator of his own adventure explaining his absence, but a witness to theirs, preparing himself to listen to what happened in his absence, in the sunlit bathroom smelling of talcum and clean porcelain: the tapestry of someone's experience woven to account for his lost time and theirs, woven and then unraveled repeatedly so that his own story might complete or replace it, if he were to return, if he were not to return, to the sunlit and mountainous island of his birth smelling of olive trees, currants, wine and the ocean wind. But the bathroom's empty. He touches the toothbrushes, and feels that two are wet. He takes three aspirin and drinks them down, washes his face and combs his hair in the spotless mirror where his eyes, suspended between past and future, hang listening between his own and others' lives for any momentary sound that might witness his presence in this story and reveal theirs. The cool spring wind blows in the open window. He looks outside and sees that one of the cars is gone from the garage. My story lacks importance now, he says.

Now he can imagine the mother and her son driving away from him, driving in any direction where he remembers there is a road. But from this point a line goes zinging upward and left in a terrific curve until a nose appears in profile with an eye, dark, primitive, animal, that gazes at the narrator and asks: "Where does this road lead that we haven't been?" Not just a Texas steer cudding the green wind and green branches of overcast spring, but an eye demanding what, in profile, is the matter with the car, the mother, the son, that they take this road in ignorance of its meaning, of what it might lead them to, toward what husband or father who is not already the son and only the son. The eye and profile in a bathroom mirror, as Picasso might have drawn it, not of a hero but of a man-animal, a story forming in his mind, whose hands are empty: the eye and profile of the driver of the car as seen, peripherally, by his companion who is looking forever ahead and not at him, as the road's future races toward them, and the collision between their going and its coming confuses the story that each has to tell: the place where he must plant his oar in the earth, and she succumb to old age, her beauty gone, and the son go on alone without companions. It is the inertia of those who wait to be moved, who have no will to move, as in the Problem of Three Bodies, where you must try and determine the motion of three bodies moving under no influence but that of their mutual gravitation (moon around earth disturbed by action of sun, earth around sun disturbed by action of Mars) and no general solution might ever be found. In springtime the will escapes, the old stories grow fresh. But who can enact them?

Habits we grow: not to answer but to neutralize the questions.

"I need help."
I offer you my help.
"No. I need help."

Three children in the spring rain, three girls, in the festival of rain, dancing a circle. They imitate nothing they know, their dance is pure feeling. They dance because they feel like it. They feel like the rain. But the eldest, the tall one, needs help with her math question, which is not a feeling like the rain but a problem she can't dance out an answer to: as the boy, driving alone with his mother away from his father, has trouble adding to three, though he knows that three is there, a feeling and not a number, a feeling and a problem he must answer. So when he goes in search of his father, among other men's stories, or tears out his bleeding eyes having learnt who his father was, from other men's stories, he is aware that his own story is something he takes part in but does not create—as this one wanders everywhere but home. The lifeline is the question, is the story. The end is the answer, is neutrality. The fetal question mark lies curled in itself like a seed, and the end is academic: a dot closing off the birth of possible ways to be seen beyond his image in the glass, where every act of his past imagined and real returns to him through his eyes, unwitnessed except by himself, the dancer in his own rain, the father out of season with his children's needs and lives.

And no general solution can ever be found. You are lost among particulars, clinging to the driftwood of what happens, describing the pattern of grain, the texture, the nail holes, with the accuracy of desperation, trying to fight against the entropy that might be your salvation, your way to Ithaka, the island kingdom where you once were king. But the star you followed was drawn by a child, its character was plastic. It has changed since then, it has hardened into a perfect geometric figure whose edges cut, cut away at space, without touching anything live. The bureaucrat returns home, drunk, from cutting at figures all day and his soul's torment all night, to find his family gone, and all his stories of Troy which he had kept to offer them as proof are now his sole possession, as the songs of Orpheus, who was torn apart because of his power to affect others, returned to the wind which was their origin, beyond human interference, the elemental spirit that leads and misleads all tellers of stories, and drives them mad.

What happened to the remaindered songs of Orpheus? Were they sold off cheap or were they pulped? We listen to the wind with the sense that we're hearing words, words of the forgotten singer we think are our own words, and write down as our words, and publish as our words. In the spring and autumn the words are particularly clear. In the heat of summer or in the winter cold the words are intermittent, they refer to no change, either of death or birth, but are words of the dimensionless present, picked up in the street or at the fireside, waiting for time to move. Or do we make the change in our lives, as the man in a Texas suburb now leaves his bathroom, walks down the stairs and gets in his car. He sits thinking for a minute or two, because his next decision is whether to go his own way or go the way he imagines the mother went with her son (as this part of the story was not foretold: that he would return to an empty house, with no one to tell his story to, and no one's story to hear) and ought he to have brought the shotgun with him, to assert his rights and prevent something from happening which the mother and her son might later regret (torn, bleeding eyes, suicide with a light cord) or did the boy take the shotgun with him, to assert his right to the mother, and prevent his father's story from having the power to influence all future stories, as it has done? In spring, we decide to return.

> The child and her mother lay down to sleep.
> Sleep, said the mother, we'll wake up soon
> In a world where nothing will hear your song,
> Where you will not have to become a woman
> And learn to repeat my life, my song.
> The child and her mother lay down and slept
> In the air too deadly to breathe for long,

And nobody found them until they were gone.

I wake up and heat a pot of coffee on the electric stove. The bitter taste of waking, sweetened with sugar, whitened with cream. The three girls are already dressed for school and ready to leave. In winter we must wake them up, in the dark and cold of a primitive house, the primitive time of year: light fires, light stoves, as we would keep it that way, "down to basics," the effort now a habit not a plan. But now it is late spring, the longest and most perfect spring in memory here, and there is a story escaping me whose truth I don't feel, of a man in search of something he must answer, some quietus for himself and for others (coffee, life, the implement at hand: the electric stove, not primitive, or subject to fatal use) as events repeat themselves long after they are understood, because the picture was not clear, the picture was unimaginable. The man in his car can't imagine where he is going, if where he is going is where the others have gone, and his effort to imagine breaks the back of whatever story he has to tell, which is not his life story or theirs, but the day's story, the story of this spring, where three girls are dancing in the grass, and there is no future beyond their dancing in the grass, no need to find the mother and her son, no Ithaka, no home. Three girls dancing in the grass, the sun caught in their hair. A hand practicing a waltz on the piano, the rhythm lost in an effort to get the notes right: moment by moment, in sequence, right, so a sentence might form, a story find its direction.

"You should have done your homework."

I need help.

This other man now, my double, my imaginary neighbor, whose fate is no longer to struggle for home over dark seas, but to go in search of those he left behind, who have left him now, his story lacking importance, and theirs about to begin without him but with him in mind—remember the way you were before you died, the dishes had to be done, the floor swept, and the garbage taken out? Something killed you in an upstairs room, and left a man escaping down the stairs with the secret of what he'd seen. The spring sunlight falls on the place where your body was found. It is not help you need but another story, telling of how you drove west and were never found, not in your identity, not with a son, but alone. There's always this threat, this demon, behind the calm faces of possible alternatives: those who read and watch and are angry because the truth follows a crueler logic than our actions can encompass, making a clown of Oedipus in his worst moment. Turn the page and you might find happiness. You might find a man to care for you, or a woman, for you as you are, in your identity, which now must be established by looking through your personal effects, or relying upon the expert testimony of your friends. Walls only bleed in movies and in dreams. The objective world follows its star the sun, and your part in it is your shadow. *Sabi, sabi*—there's only so much a person can do, like Basho leaving a handful of rice for the child he found abandoned on the road, and moving on, moving north, an old man headed for his own death, the planting of his oar in foreign soil. Leaving his house and going out on foot, when age had come upon him, to meet his end far from home, to keep his shadow moving at all costs until the very end, unencumbered by that child he couldn't take with him for it was only his shadow and himself, walking on, waiting for some place to claim them finally. So this man is free to leave his house and go on alone, or he is free to go and look for those others whose absence makes him feel lonely, guilty and afraid—wishing the car would decide for him, as feet have a way of doing, when the mind is uncertain. What would you do if faced with this decision? Who knows, they might have gone shopping. Who knows. Who knows.

He bores me, this man and his problems. He hasn't star quality. He lacks the vision to return or stay away, he deserves no story, and I can't ever tell what he wants. My neighbor doesn't even know his own name. "We can always choose," I told him one day earlier this spring as he sat in his car looking lost, but he just nodded and stared straight ahead, as if it were the direction and not the motion that was important: the windshield a telescope fixed on a star not yet formed, a vision so distant and vague it had not yet the gravity to draw him on. I watched him sit there throughout the spring and into what is now early summer. I took him food, I talked to him about the necessity of divorce, of forgetting the mother and son who had probably forgotten him. I brought him his mail, and began to pay his bills by forging his name on his own checks, until the forgeries became apparent as I didn't know his name and he wouldn't help me. I tried to explain our double role in this to the police and the newspapers, but all I got was more unwelcome personal attention for one who, being in part his creator now, should have concealed himself and let the man speak for himself, develop some character and decide to act. But he just sits there, the ignition key in his hand, the battery slowly dying in front of him. I talk to him about Orpheus, Odysseus, Oedipus, trying to fill in his past and give him some patterns to move with: but the details of the stories do not fit his memory, which is very literal, as a Texan's must be if he is to get on in the real world. Dealing with him has begun to affect my powers of imagination. I find I must stick to facts at the expense of my own visions, and am being dragged down to his own level of pitiable inertia, while the lovely spring has passed and left me standing at the open window of his car, sweating, resentful, and nervous for my own sanity. I try and tell him that the mother and son who abandoned him will return if he sits here long enough, if only as the report of an accident or a demand for funds sent by a remote lawyer. But he pays no attention. He'll neither stay in his house nor drive away in his car. It is I who must abandon him now and retrieve my self, wherever it has gone, alone or in whatever company.

But I keep seeing a mother driving west, telling me about her child, her son or daughter, lost in time behind or in time ahead. They may be an idea or they may be real, figments of starlight or the stars themselves, so much farther away than the ghosts they make dance in the grass. Fewer and fewer babies slip through into the rubber surgical gloves of waiting doctors. Soon there will be three grandmothers dancing in the grass, full of the signs of spring, of continuing promise of life, and the ghost dance of Wovoka will be universal, though the children in the mountain may not be aware of it, in their separate kingdom in the haunted mountain. They say Telemachus may have married Circe and had children by her: or he married Circe's daughter, killed Circe in an argument and was killed by his wife, her daughter: either of which is a fitting response to his father's life, a lesson in filial devotion or even obsession, the story's gravity drawing him back and away from Penelope towards that other star, mistaken or not, ignorant or not, the need to complete the tapestry his mother never finished. Which may be why this father sits there wondering what to do, staring through the windshield at a vision he cannot recognize or name: the key in his hand, the power at his foot, but the battery gone dead in front of him. He doesn't know those stories and he doesn't remember his own: he has nothing to go on, no star to guide him. Should I leave him alone and call him typical? Or should I leave him alone and call him an unfortunate isolated case, the victim of a great misunderstanding, whose face doesn't even emerge here, who has done nothing to merit our attention at all. He has gone blind, and must hobble his way on a stick to the sacred grove. He has lost his power to sing the great songs that destroy the singer, the impassioned songs that make the animals listen and, eventually, hell itself claim him back. He is a taxi driver in a world of nameless ghosts.

But none of this is good enough. The spring rains have come and gone. The clouds continue to blow in from the Gulf, the low humid clouds of early summer that sweat but never rain: neither mind nor world feels right, they irritate each other, their relationship is intensely uneasy, the one sucking the other's breath, the other fighting to keep it. "When did we last make love?" is the landscape's question, in the trickling sunlight of early June driving west past these hills, knowing the journey is a short one, a relief from the heat of the house, to which the question returns us, answering itself or not, depending on what preoccupations meet us at the door and claim the time we want to set aside for each other—an endless foreplay of necessities amounting to a journey never quite complete, the censored scene in Penelope's bedroom after both had undergone the tests each had invented to make sure. A man and a woman alone now in their house, and those who were part of their story, who died or were left behind, not less than they but no longer the subject now, no longer what the story is about or where it is going, despite memories and dreams which last far longer than the ones whose lives they preserve, which are like waves that push you forward and drag you back until eventually you are washed up exhausted on some beach which proves to be the shore of your own island, the doorstep of your home, with a story of your own to tell and an ear to listen to others, once you have got your strength back and are able to stagger uphill or upstairs, inland to find and create the fate that was promised you, whether the ones you expected to find are there or not, whether or not the ones you find are the same ones you expected, who know or have forgotten your identity and name.

> Brother, it's all in the mind, I tell you.
> Dance it out in the grass.
> Dance, dance until your ghost returns.

But that is not good enough either, not even if memorized and sung repeatedly. There are dimensions and footfalls not accounted for by magic chants invented on the spot. You move, I move, we move, in a parody of the dance our children make. The sentences that must be perfect, the lines that must scan or be meaningless! The precise, beautiful techniques that lead to orgasm, or to disappointment. Such is art, Orpheus—what was your secret? What song could release the spirit of the man who is afraid to drive his car? A lullaby, a psychiatrist's love and attention. *The big horse would not drink water. Injured legs, frozen mane, would not touch the wet of the shore. Flies on his muzzle, the dead river pressing his throat, the agony of snow, wild horse of daybreak. The horse begins to cry, he whinnies towards the mountains. Don't come in! Run to the mountains, the grey valleys where the mare stands waiting. The big horse who wouldn't drink water, the horse beginning to cry.* So the failure to maintain seriousness, seriousness that might lead to acts of suicide or acts of splendor: a prose trot of a Spanish lullaby with bits left out: sketches of a condition where nothing happens but much is imagined, as if future stories cold be composed from these possibilities—or else the story is here, all that it will ever be, already told, as spring passing into summer and now this terrible heat wave demands another sort of words and nerves, a man perhaps unable not to move, as all around him is the still and increasing heat of a greater paralysis than his own. They used to pay a storyteller, a singer, for his time, and his inspiration was their need of him. Five hundred years ago

> *¡Que permanezca la tierra!*
> *¡Que estén en pie los montes!*
> *Así venía hablando Ayocuan Cuetzpaltzin.*
> *En Tlaxcala, en Huexotzinco*
> *Que se repartan*
> *flores de maíz tostado, flores de cacao.*
> *¡Que permanezca la tierra!*

was the song of the Aztec poet Ayocuan Cuetzpaltzin, the savant, the white eagle, of Tecamachalco. He sang of the fruitful earth, of toasted maize—popcorn—and cocoa flowers, the plentiful and permanent earth, the standing mountains. The poem is also a prayer against catastrophes remembered and foretold. That the earth not come to an end, the old cycles of the long Aztec year continue as before, the new calendar wheel beginning every fifty-two years with the ceremony of new fire on the Hill of the Star at Culhuacan, no longer a center of power then at the time the poet sang, who was born in mid-century perhaps during the great crop-failures of those years, the five unlucky calendar days stretching to five years of famine and death. The god who is always inventing himself offers no promise of the shape of things. In the bland eyes of the man frozen at the start of the journey he cannot make, these thoughts remain, however vague, an older promise and fear beyond the faces he would search for, bring home, leave home, to recover the meaning of his own microscopic dot on earth: the passion of words open to the sky, beyond contradiction, where he last made love and now tries to imagine the place where it might have happened. It has been a long flirtation, his waiting here. Erotic dreams, words feeling between the legs of words, brief affairs intense this side of childbirth, the freedom to eat the seed before the seed has grown. A mother leading her child into death, inventing and singing a lullaby to quiet its fears. A man waiting to be told what road to take, as a visitor at that grave, his own daughters growing tall in the high Texas sun whose heat eats out the centers of his days. Flowers of cocoa, popcorn flowers— *¡Que se repartan!* Time now to let you drive for a while, face beside me, companion who waits between sleep and restlessness, to take control. The child's amoeba star is drawn but never finished. It has the shape of its maker's imagination, the blind and ageless audacity of this hand to finish what it has begun without end: to construct, in the permanent shadow of a moving cloud, this house where people live.

David Wevill was born a Canadian in Yokohama, Japan, where his family had been living for two generations, in 1935. He left for Canada before the outbreak of World War II, moved to England during the 1950s, read History and English at Caius College, Cambridge, and gained a reputation as a premier young poet during his association with the London-based literary collective The Group. Wevill moved to Texas in the late 1960s, where he co-edited *Delos: A Journal on and of Translation* and taught at the University of Texas at Austin until his retirement. The author of sixteen books, his poetry was first showcased in the Penguin Modern Poets series and has since been awarded with an Arts Council Book Prize, the Richard Hillary Prize, two Arts Council Poetry Bursaries, an E.C. Gregory Trust Award, and a Guggenheim Fellowship. His work has appeared in numerous publications, including *The New York Times*, *The New Yorker*, *Poetry* (Chicago), *Harper's*, *The Listener*, *The Observer*, *The Spectator*, and on the BBC. Wevill lives in Austin, Texas.

COLOPHON

This book was designed and typeset by Michael McGriff. The text is set in Garamond, an old-style serif typeface named for the punch-cutter Claude Garamond (c. 1480 – 1561). The titles are set in Cochin, a serif typeface designed by George Peignot and named after the French engraver Charles Nicolas Cochin (1715 – 1790). The cover is set in Charlemagne and Eurostile, contemporary fonts designed by Carol Twombly and Alessandro Butti, respectively. Printed on archival-quality paper at McNaughton & Gunn, Inc.

In this edition, five copies have been hand-bound into cloth-covered boards by Carl Adamshick. These copies are numbered and signed by the author.